Companioning the Grieving Child

CURRICULUM BOOK

ACTIVITIES TO HELP CHILDREN & TEENS HEAL

PATRICIA MORRISSEY, M.S. ED.

FOREWORD BY ALAN D. WOLFELT, PH.D.

Companion Press is dedicated to the education and support of both the bereaved and breavement caregivers. We believe that those who companion the bereaved by walking with them as they journey in grief have a wonderous opportunity: to help others embrace and grow through grief—and to lead fuller, more deeply lived lives themselves because of this important ministry.

For a complete catalog and ordering information, write or call or visit our website.

Companion
PRESS

Companion Press
The Center for Loss and Life Transition

3735 Broken Bow Road | Fort Collins, CO 80526

Phone: (970) 226-6050 | Fax: 1-800-922-6051

drwolfelt@centerforloss.com | www.centerforloss.com

Companion Press is an imprint of the Center for Loss and Life Transition
3735 Broken Bow Road, Fort Collins, CO 80526
(970) 226-6050
www.centerforloss.com

Companion Press books may be purchased in bulk for sale promotions, premiums, or fundraisers. Please contact the publisher at the above address for more information.

Printed in the United States of America

18   17   16   15   14   13   5   4   3   2   1

ISBN 978-1-61722-185-9

To my sister, Mimi, and her children,
Liz, Arran, and Sean.

In 1994, Mimi and my nieces and nephew experienced
the sudden death of their husband and father, Bob Burpee.
Their strength, wisdom, and courage taught me so
much about the journey of grief.

Contents

Foreword

There is no ministry more important than companioning grieving children.

Receiving and accepting help from others is essential for *all* of us when we are in mourning, but grieving children and teens especially need and deserve our compassionate support. As with so many other things in their young lives, their early experiences with death and grief will teach them the "rules" of mourning. Is it acceptable to show others their sadness? If they're angry, will they get in trouble? Is it OK to openly ask all the questions roiling inside them?

In our mourning-avoidant culture, too often children and teens are taught to deny or repress their grief. Thank goodness for compassionate grief companions like Pat Morrissey and you. With your help, grieving children and teens can learn the truth: that grief is a normal and necessary process, and that healing and a life bursting with love are made possible by open and honest mourning.

The activities in this wonderful curriculum are designed for children's and teens' grief group leaders to use in their meetings. When we are grieving, all of us—adults included—benefit from *doing something* with our thoughts and feelings. Words are often inadequate when it comes to death and loss, so activities that engage our bodies and brains in ritual or play give us a structure for expressing ourselves. Kids, especially, respond to play and are more likely to communicate (through behaviors as well as words) while they are engaged in a game or art.

You'll note that the curriculum activities are structured around my concept of the six needs of mourning. As grief companions, our job description is anchored, in part, in creating hospitality for children to dose themselves on these six needs. The activities provide focused opportunities to do just that.

As you work with the grieving children in your care, I encourage you to observe as much as facilitate the activities. The companioning model of grief care, which I created some years ago, is anchored in a "teach me" perspective. It is about learning and observing. In fact, the meaning of "observance" comes to us from ritual. It means not only to "watch out for" but also to "keep and honor," or "to bear witness." The caregiver's awareness of this need to learn is the essence of true companioning.

Because, as Pat reminds us throughout this book, the activities themselves are not the primary purpose of each group meeting. They are but a means to an end. Always the most important goal is to create a safe place in which kids can express their grief and connect with one another. So bear witness to what is happening to the children as you work on an activity. Let them teach you what they want to do and talk about. The activity is simply a doorway. If you let them, they will create what is on the other side of that doorway with only minimal guidance from you.

"Children are resilient," people often say. In my work with hundreds of grieving children and as a father to my own three kids, I have seen that is true. But if they aren't guided by supportive adults who teach them what it means to openly and honestly mourn, too often their natural resilience walls in their grief. They "keep their chins up" and are "strong" on the outside, all the while hiding the painful, tender truth of their grief on the inside.

Thank you for being a companion to grieving children and teens. I am humbled by your devotion to creating safe places for kids to mourn. The world needs more of you.

Alan D. Wolfelt

Acknowledgments

Thank you from the bottom of my heart to all of you who have contributed to the development of *The Companioning the Grieving Child Curriculum Book*. Writing this book has been such a fulfilling project, especially the portions that deal with relating the experience of the death to a context of meaning. My understanding of this spiritual realm of death has grown tremendously.

Blessings to my sister, Mimi, whose husband died at age 42 in 1994, leaving her with three children, Liz (11), Arran (9), and Sean (7). From the beginning of this tragic death and through all these years, each of you has modeled your journey of grief with an internal source of strength and found meaning, purpose, and the ability to live and love life fully again. Thank you for your commendable fortitude, courage, support of each other, and inspiration. Also much appreciation for introducing me to Ele's Place, where they opened their hearts to you and your family and opened my eyes to the power of a grief center.

A huge note of gratitude to Alan Wolfelt for his compassionate words and books about companioning the bereaved. Thank you, especially, for endorsing my work and this book.

Thank you to MargaretAnn's Place in Milwaukee for teaching me so much about children and grief. Through your mentorship and my experience, I learned so much about the importance of a structured grief curriculum. A special acknowledgment to Debra Smith-Anderson, Ginger Heigl, and Nichole Schwerman for your time, resources, and education.

I so appreciate the Southeast Wisconsin Grief Network, whose mission is to support and companion the bereaved and the community through their representation of hospitals, hospices, grief centers, churches, and funeral homes. They model leadership for those who companion the bereaved through education, care, and compassion.

The families and volunteers at Mourning Cloak are always dear to my heart. To the volunteers, a sincere thank you for your continual support of our grieving families and for always opening up your hearts. For our families, you continually amaze me with your courage, fortitude, and openness. I have learned so much from each of you.

To my son, Mike, and daughter, Joy, I so appreciate your support and your "cheerleading." You have been my biggest advocates and are always a source of strength. I love you so much!

My entire Morrissey family continues to buoy me, especially when large decisions need to be made. Thank you for your concern and love.

I'm grateful to my sister-in-law, Susan, who spent countless hours with me as I blazed the IRS trail to turn Mourning Cloak into a 501(c)(3) organization. Thankfully, and with much love, this happened!!

And what is life without dear friends! A special recognition to Dooley Vogel and Mary Hickey for always being there for me and for encouraging me with this venture. I love you both!

Finally, to my husband, Tom, for his constant wisdom, inspiration, love, support, and compassion, especially during the time I have been working on this book. I am blessed to be married to a man who not only understands grief but exemplifies and embraces gratefulness towards life and love. You are the best!

Introduction

"If the shoe doesn't fit, must we change the foot?"
GLORIA STEINEM

Instead, let's change the shoe. Let's dig deeper into developing a grief curriculum that is well structured, well done, and brain- and outcome-based, with goals and objectives that match age. We'll need to ask questions: What is the purpose of this lesson? How can it be better organized? How can we determine if the purposes are being met?

To help answer these questions, let's turn to Alan D. Wolfelt, Ph.D. Dr. Wolfelt is a grief counselor and the director of the Center for Loss and Life Transition in Fort Collins, Colorado. He presents a well-researched model of grief for children and teens that emphasizes grief as a process in his book *Companioning the Grieving Child: A Soulful Guide for Caregivers*. In it he covers his six reconciliation needs of mourning, which are yield signs that a grieving person is likely to encounter on his or her journey through grief. Each need is presented below in the context of helping grieving children and teens.

1. **Acknowledging the reality of the death** involves helping the children and teens gently confront the truth about the death and recognize that the person who died will never physically be in their lives again. Children and teens need open, honest, clear, and developmentally appropriate information about the nature and cause of the death. They can only cope with what they know; they cannot cope with what they do not know.

   In addition, a child may need help understanding what death means (that the body has stopped working and the person will never see, breathe, or talk again). The ability to acknowledge the reality of the death only comes about after the child has had opportunities to talk out, play out, and even act out the circumstances of the death. This may take several months and will require the gentle support of a significant adult who can accept the child's need to confront the reality some of the time while pushing it away at other times.

2. **Embracing the pain of the loss** involves encouraging and allowing the children and teens to move toward and embrace their many thoughts and feelings after a death. Caring adults often want to protect bereaved children by avoiding talk about the death, but children need to know that it is OK to experience and express their feelings of grief.

   In addition, children and teens need the security of being nurtured and knowing that their physical, emotional, and spiritual needs will continue to be met despite the major changes that have occurred.

3. **Remembering the person who died** involves encouraging the children to move from a "here and now" relationship to the people who died to a "what was." In order to heal, the children and teens must convert their relationships with the people who died from a relationship of presence to one of memory.

   Caregivers can help facilitate this need by encouraging the children to share memories and dreams of the people who died. Children may also work through this need by creating memory books, carrying keepsakes or photographs of the deceased, and participating in family memorial rituals. Remembering makes hope possible. As children or teens embrace the past, they become open to new experiences and relationships.

4. **Developing a new self-identity** involves helping the children discover self-identities apart from the people who died. The roles played by the people who died are critical in children's self-definitions, so when a family member or friend dies, their identities are permanently changed. As well, the social and functional roles in the children's family or peer groups change (who cooks dinner each night or who is the child's confidante). Therefore children are mourning not only the losses on the outside, but those on the inside, too.

   As children and teens redefine their identities, they may act in ways that are unfamiliar as they try on new identities. It is critical to support the children and teens as they work through this need of mourning or their development may be hindered. On the brighter side, however, many bereaved children evolve more compassionate self-identities as a result of their losses.

5. **Searching for meaning** involves allowing and encouraging the children to ask "Why" and "How" questions after someone they love has died. As a caregiver, be aware that you do not have to have all the answers, and, in fact, admitting that you don't know can be very helpful! Children and teens are likely to ask many questions of adults they trust, sometimes repeating questions even if they have already been answered. Keep answering their questions.

   Sometimes children and teens do not verbalize this search for meaning but demonstrate it in art, play, or acting-out behaviors. The children may appear to be truly suffering as they go through this search for meaning but with patience, support, and understanding from caring adults, they will find continued meaning in their lives and accept that there are things in our lives that we cannot know and cannot have control over.

6. **Receiving ongoing support from adults** involves ensuring that caring adult presences are available to the children, even long after a death. Even those children and teens who actively participate in the work of mourning will still mourn the loss in different ways as they pass through various developmental stages and on into adulthood. Adult caregivers can facilitate this mourning need by appreciating the impact of loss on children and teens and allowing and encouraging a child to mourn long after the death.

By working through each of these needs with the help of supportive adults, children and teens will be able to reconcile their losses. Dr. Wolfelt defines reconciliation as "what occurs when the mourner works to integrate the new reality of moving forward in life without the physical presence of the person who died." Reconciliation brings with it a renewed sense of energy and confidence and an ability to fully acknowledge the reality of the death and to reconnect with the activities of living.

As well as following Dr. Wolfelt's six reconciliation needs, this book also makes use of his companioning model, from his book

Companioning the Bereaved. The word *companion,* when broken down into its original Latin roots, means *com* for "with" and *pan* for "bread." This means that when working with the bereaved, it is comparable to sharing a meal with a friend or equal. Dr. Wolfelt offers 11 tenets when companioning the bereaved:

1. Companioning is about being present to another person's pain; it is not about taking away the pain.

2. Companioning is about going to the wilderness of the soul with another human being; it is not about thinking you are responsible for finding the way out.

3. Companioning is about honoring the spirit; it is not about focusing on the intellect.

4. Companioning is about listening with the heart; it is not about analyzing with the head.

5. Companioning is about bearing witness to the struggles of others; it is not about judging or directing these struggles.

6. Companioning is about walking alongside; it is not about leading.

7. Companioning is about discovering the gifts of sacred silence; it is not about filling up every moment with words.

8. Companioning is about being still; it is not about frantic movement forward.

9. Companioning is about respecting disorder and confusion; it is not about imposing order and logic.

10. Companioning is about learning from others; it is not about teaching them.

11. Companioning is about compassionate curiosity; it is not about expertise.

When working with grieving children, you must create a safe place where they can embrace their feelings of loss. Do not profess to have all the answers, but open your heart and mind and the children will teach you about their own unique grief.

The Companioning the Grieving Child Curriculum Book: Activities to Help Children & Teens Heal is meant to assist grieving children individually or integrate within an existing grief support program for children and teens that already contains goals, objectives, and outcome-based assessments. If your program does not already include these things, I recommend adding them. Each activity here begins with a goal and objective to gently guide the time you spend with the children, making the most of your time together.

For most children, death is a new experience. And like all new experiences, the unknown can be confusing and frightening. Most children do not know what to expect following the loss of a family member or friend. Young children may not understand what death really means and may be confused or even frightened by the reactions of other family members. In the case of traumatic death, the confusion and fear is even greater.

For adults, death is more familiar and the grieving process is something many adults know first-hand. Most adults have experienced the range of feelings that often come with traumatic loss—anger, confusion, and sadness—and have learned ways to cope with loss. This may not be the case for children, particularly young children.

At the same time, children will seek answers and comfort from their caregivers and other adults in their lives. Yet in the face of traumatic death, adults often feel helpless in this role. While adults cannot have answers to all the questions that children may have about death, they can help children better understand the grieving process.

Children should always be involved in the grieving process. They are much better off when their grief is acknowledged and they are allowed to mourn in the company of family, friends, and support groups. Explaining Dr. Wolfelt's six needs of mourning to children, at their developmental level, is important so that they begin to understand this grieving process.

How to Use this Book

The Companioning the Grieving Child Curriculum Book incorporates the theme of butterflies, as they also companion us. Through their metamorphosis, they are a symbol of faith. They beckon the bereaved to keep their faith as they undergo transitions in their own lives.

This curriculum book is divided into six sections, one for each of the six reconciliation needs. For each of these needs, I have chosen a specific butterfly as a symbol. You will find the corresponding butterfly throughout each section, and the introduction to each section's need will describe the butterfly and detail how it relates to the need.

There are four activities in every section for early childhood (developmental ages 4 – 7), elementary (developmental ages 8 – 12), and teens. These activities are designed for developmental ages; therefore, please use your professional judgment to determine which activities would be best suited for the children and teens in your program. Remember, there is a difference between developmental and chronological age: chronological age is determined by time and developmental age is an expression of a child's or teen's maturational progress.

Each section contains an objective and each lesson contains a goal. The goal is always specific to the activity and the objective always relates to one of the six reconciliation needs. By discussing the specific reconciliation need before the lesson begins, children will have a better conceptual idea of the lesson. Once the activity is completed, it is important to once again go back to the reconciliation need and ask the children and teens how they think that the activity related to the specific need.

Many of the lessons contain art and music projects. Since only seven percent of our communication is verbal, it is important that children be able to communicate their thoughts and feelings through such things as art, music, writing, and drama. Grieving children need confidence so that they can regain their self-image. Often, nonverbal expressions might be an easier way for some children to cope and share their stories.

Before using any of these lessons, it is advised that the facilitator actually work through the activity. If the activity includes a book, find it in your resource center or order it from a trusted source. The source listed next to the book in the activity is where it is most easily found. Read the book before the group meets, thinking of some questions that you might want to ask the children or teens after the reading.

If there are worksheets needed, you will find them on the website for the Center for Loss at www.centerforloss.com/downloads. All of the activities are available as a downloadable PDF document so you can print off as many copies of a page as you need.

Make sure that the required materials for each lesson are close at hand. Create a model of the activity ahead of time, so that you are familiar with the directions. This way you can give some important first-hand tips on the project. Also, be ready to let the children or teens know what they can do when their project is completed, as they will all finish at different rates. At the end of the session, relate this project back to the reconciliation need and see what connections the children and teens can make. Remember to let them teach you!

I always use an icebreaker to start each lesson, as they can be a positive beginning by energizing the group, initiating creative thinking, and encouraging involvement. You may choose from any of the icebreakers listed toward the back of the book or search the internet for more options.

Also, please note that in the introduction to each need is printed, *"Always think of the activity as the secondary task to accomplish for the group. The first task is getting the group members to express grief and connect with each other. The game or activity is always just a medium through which these tasks may be accomplished."* This is crucial to remember for those who companion the bereaved because the specific needs of the children and teens are the main purpose of a grief support group.

The last pages of this book list the books, games, and other materials that you will need if you decide to implement this entire curriculum. They are organized alphabetically by type (book, game, website, and other) to aid easy access.

As of the time of publication, all books and games were available at the places given and all the websites were functional. Due to the shifting nature of the internet, you may find that the link provided does not work in the future. In that event, an internet search with as many details as possible should furnish you with the new link or a new but similar resource.

I am hopeful that the activities in this book will enhance your grief support program. If you would like to comment on any of the activities, please email me at pat@mourningcloak.org. Thank you!!

Acknowledge the reality of the death

This first need of mourning involves gently helping children or teens face the reality that someone they love or care about will never physically come back into their lives again.

Whether the death was sudden or anticipated, acknowledging the full reality of the loss may occur over weeks and months. To survive, children or teens may try to push away the reality of the death at times. They may discover themselves replaying events surrounding the death and confronting memories, both good and bad. This replay is a very important part of this need of mourning. It's as if each time they talk it out, the event is a little more real.

This need of mourning, just like the other five that follow, may intermittently require attention for months. Remind the children or teens to be patient and kind to themselves as they work on facing the reality of the deaths.

The activities in this section are designed to assist children and teens in telling their stories about the deaths of the people who died and understanding the concept of death. As the facilitator, you will be answering their questions truthfully and helping them know and understand their grief rights.

Companioning you in the first need of mourning is the great spangled fritillary. This butterfly represents the reality that, after metamorphosis, a butterfly cannot return to being a caterpillar, just like children and teens must acknowledge the reality that someone loved has died and their lives will never be the same again.

Remember to always think of the activity as the secondary task to accomplish for the group. The first task is to get the group members to express their grief and connect with each other. The game or activity is just a medium through which these tasks may be accomplished.

MATERIALS:

I Heard Your Daddy Died by Mark Scrivani, available from the Centering Corporation

Copies of the *"I Heard Your _____ Died"* worksheet

centerforloss.com
Worksheets.pdf
Pages 1 - 3

Colored pencils

I Heard Your Daddy Died

GOAL:

To get to know the children in your group and have them talk briefly about the deaths and their stories

ACTIVITY:

1. Ask each child his or her name, who died, and how he or she is feeling about the death. Is there anything else he or she would like to share about the death?

2. Read aloud the book *I Heard Your Daddy Died*. Take time and talk about the pictures when you are reading the book out loud.

3. Ask the following questions after reading the book:

   • What feelings have you had after the death?

   • How are feelings of sadness shown? How have you shown that you were or still are sad?

   • Is it OK to be lonely or angry? When have you felt this way? What things can you do when you are lonely or sad?

   • Do you have special memories of your mommy (or daddy, brother, or sister)? What things can you do to keep these memories?

   • Where do you think whoever died is? Is he or she in your heart?

4. Hand out the *"I Heard Your _____ Died"* memory sheet. Have the kids complete this sheet using colored pencils and then share their answers.

Gentle Willow

Young children wonder what happens when someone is dying or has died. This is very normal and deserves a truthful answer.

GOAL:

To help young children grasp the concept of death and dying by looking at what happens in nature

ACTIVITY:

1. Discuss with the group what they think death is. Write down each of their ideas on a large sheet of paper.

2. Read aloud and discuss *Gentle Willow*.

3. Discuss how Little Tree helped Amanda and how Amanda helped Gentle Willow.

4. Look back at their paper and see if they want to add any other words.

5. Ask the children what kind words and actions were expressed to them after the deaths.

6. Make little trees with the children using brown and green clay.

7. When they have made their trees, ask them what words they might want to hang on their trees that are words of kindness, such as nice, love, smile, hugs, kisses, listen, hope, etc. Use magnetic poetry words and wire to attach these to the trees. Alternately, you can write the words on small pieces of paper and attach them with wire or string.

8. Ask the children how they think their trees might be used for themselves and others.

AGE GROUP:

Early Childhood

MATERIALS:

Large sheet of paper

Markers

Gentle Willow by Joyce C. Mills, available from Amazon

Brown and green clay

Magnetic poetry words or small pieces of paper

Magnetic wire or string

Early Childhood

MATERIALS:

Lifetimes by Bryan Mellonie, available from Amazon

One colored sock per child (the thicker the better)

Needle and thread

Two clothespins

Two Ping-Pong balls per puppet

Markers

Glue, preferably hot glue

Black felt

Yarn

Scissors

Grief Sock Puppets

It is difficult for many young children to talk directly about death. It may be easier for them to open up through indirect methods.

GOAL:

To use puppets to ease the fear of talking directly about death and allow the children to express their thoughts

ACTIVITY:

1. Before your session, make sock puppets for each child, following the directions on the next page.

2. Before reading *Lifetimes* with the children, talk about how insects, birds, plants, fish, and people can only live one lifetime. Some live short lives and others live long lives.

3. Read aloud *Lifetimes*.

4. Discuss the beginnings (births) and endings (deaths) that all living things have. Can the children give examples of living things that have a short lifetime or a long lifetime? Some examples may be that some insects only live a few hours or days or that birds can live from one or two to 50 years or that people can live a few hours or 100 years.

5. Using the puppets, encourage a discussion of one of the following topics:

   • Reactions to being told of the deaths.

   • Last memories of the people who died.

   • How the children are feeling tonight.

   • Special memories with their loved ones.

INSTRUCTIONS:

1. Thread the needle and tie thread in a knot. Put the sock on your hand with your fingers in the toe and the back of your wrist at the heel. With your hand in the shape of the letter 'C', push the toe of the sock between your fingers and thumb, toward your palm.

2. Mark the cheeks with the clothespins and hold them in place by stitching an 'X' into each cheek. Remove the clothespins.

3. Put the sock back on your hand and mark where you want the eyes to be with a marker. Remove the sock and hot glue your Ping-Pong balls onto the sock where you marked it.

4. Cut two small circles out of felt for the pupils of the eyes. Hot glue these onto the Ping-Pong balls.

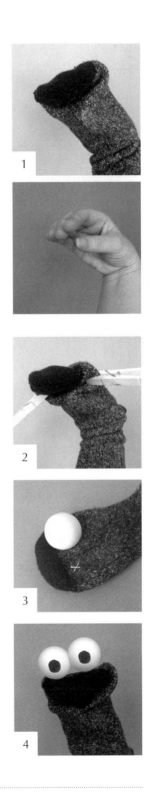

MATERIALS:

My, Oh My—A Butter-fly!: All About Butterflies (Cat in the Hat's Learning Library), available from Amazon

"Life Cycle of a Butterfly" worksheet

centerforloss.com
Worksheets.pdf
Page 4

Five-inch squares of different colored tissue paper

Pipe cleaners

String or fishing line

Wire hangers

The Wonder of Butterflies

Butterflies are an ideal way to explain that death is a part of life since the average lifespan of a butterfly is about a month.

GOAL:

To explain the concept of life and death using the metamorphosis of a butterfly

ACTIVITY:

1. Read aloud and discuss *My, Oh My—A Butterfly!: All About Butterflies*.

2. Show them the "Life Cycle of a Butterfly" handout and talk through a butterfly's lifespan, highlighting that most butterflies live and die within a month. (For more information about butterflies, visit www.kidsbutterfly.org.)

3. Make tissue paper butterflies with the children, following the instructions below.

4. When the butterflies are completed, ask the children what these butterflies are going to represent to them. How can these butterflies help them with the deaths of their loved ones?

INSTRUCTIONS

1. Stack two tissue squares, then trim the edges to resemble wings.

1

2. Fold the pipe cleaner in half over the wings, as shown, bunching the tissue slightly.

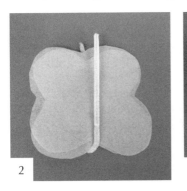

2

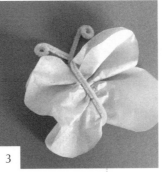

3

3. Twist together the pipe cleaner ends to hold the paper in place. Then curl the pipe cleaner tips around your finger or a pencil to create antennae.

4. Tie one end of the string or fishing line to the pipe cleaner body near the head and the other end to a wire hanger. With another piece of string or fishing wire, tie one end to the tail of the body and the other end to the wire hanger.

4

Elementary

MATERIALS:

Copies of the *"Missing the Five Senses of My Loved One"* worksheet

centerforloss.com
Worksheets.pdf
Page 5

Colored pencils, crayons, or markers

When I Miss You by Cornelia Maude Spelman, available from Amazon

Sense A Bility game, available from Amazon

How I Miss My Loved One's Sight, Sound, Touch, Smell, and Foods!

When someone loved dies, a child misses every part of this person—what he or she looked like, sounded like, felt like, smelled like, and even some of his or her favorite foods.

GOAL:

To acknowledge and remember the person who died through the child's five senses

ACTIVITY:

1. Talk with the children about the people who died.

2. Have the children fill in the different senses on the "Missing the Five Senses" worksheet with words and pictures about what they miss most about each sense when they think about the people who died. Encourage the children to share some of what they wrote with the rest of the group.

3. Read aloud and discuss the book *When I Miss You*.

4. If time remains, play the game Sense A Bility.

I Have So Many Questions

When children ask questions about death, it is sometimes difficult to know how to respond. There are no "perfect" answers—the most important thing is to answer the children's questions as patiently and gently as possible and to understand that their concerns and reactions will be different from yours. Expect to have to repeat the answers over and over again and to provide details if a child asks for them.

GOAL:
To provide children with a safe place to ask questions about death and receive answers

ACTIVITY:
1. Ahead of time, print out "Children's Questions About Death" and the "I Have So Many Questions About Death" game board and glue them to index cards and construction paper, respectively.

2. Read aloud *Where Do People Go When They Die?*.

3. Discuss with the kids some of the questions they have about death.

4. Hand out one game board to each child.

5. The youngest person begins the game.

6. Roll one die and advance that many spaces. When they land on a space, they must follow the directions on the space (if any) and read a facedown card. The question should first be answered by the player and then opened up to the other players. If a child cannot answer a question, then allow another child to answer for him. As a facilitator, add additional information or questions when appropriate.

7. The person who has exactly the correct die number to reach the end is the winner.

8. If time permits, shuffle the question cards and play the game again.

AGE GROUP:
Elementary

MATERIALS:

Where Do People Go When They Die? by Mindy Avra Portnoy, available from Amazon

Copies of the *"I Have So Many Questions About Death"* game board worksheet

 centerforloss.com
Worksheets.pdf
Pages 6 - 7

Colored 9" x 12" pieces of construction paper

Glue

"Children's Questions About Death" worksheet

 centerforloss.com
Worksheets.pdf
Page 8

Index cards

One game piece for each child (try using pieces from Monopoly, Sorry, the Game of Life, or other games)

One die

Elementary

What to Do When You Worry Too Much: A Kid's Guide to Overcoming Anxiety by Dawn Huebner, available from Amazon

Directions for making Butterfly Sun Catchers, available from spoonful. com/crafts/butterfly-sun-catcher

Tissue paper in several colors

White glue

8 ½" x 11" black foam sheet (black construc-tion paper or cardstock can also be used)

8 ½" x 11" heavy white paper

Pencils

Scissors

Clear tape or fishing line

Googly eyes (optional)

If Only…

Many times when children experience the death of someone loved, they feel that "if only" they had done or not done something, the person would still be alive. This feeling of guilt may be intermingled with all the other myriad feelings associated with grief.

GOAL:

To help children acknowledge that the death was not their fault and help allay some of the feelings of guilt they may have

ACTIVITY:

1. Talk about the experience of the death of their loved ones. Gently ask about and discuss the feelings of "if only." Be aware that not all of the children will have this feeling.

2. Read and discuss *What to Do When You Worry Too Much: A Kid's Guide to Overcoming Anxiety* from the What to Do Guides for Kids.

3. Talk openly with the children about how worrisome feelings can grow.

4. Talk about butterflies as a sign of hope. Explain that they are going to make a sun catcher butterfly so that if and when they are feeling guilty about the death, they can look at this butterfly, highlighted by the sun, and remind themselves that it's not their fault.

5. Use the instructions found on spoonful.com to create sun catchers with the children.

Water Bugs and Dragonflies

For children, acknowledging the death of a loved one may take weeks or months. This only happens when the child has had opportunities to talk out and play out the circumstances of the death.

GOAL:
To encourage children to talk and play out the circumstances of the deaths

ACTIVITY:
1. Talk with the children about the circumstances of the deaths of their loved ones. Encourage other group members to ask questions.

2. Read aloud and discuss the book *Water Bugs and Dragonflies* by Doris Stickney.

3. Hand out the coloring books or pages, allowing the children time to paint or color the pictures.

4. End this session by playing the Doggone Grief game.

AGE GROUP:
Elementary

MATERIALS:

Water Bugs and Dragonflies by Doris Stickney, available from Amazon

"*Water Bugs and Dragonflies*" coloring books, available from barnesandnoble.com or print free coloring pages of dragonflies from online

Watercolors, colored pencils, crayons, or markers

Doggone Grief game, available from Compassion Books

AGE GROUP:

Teens

MATERIALS:

Copies of *"Understanding Your Six Needs of Mourning for Teens"* worksheet

centerforloss.com
Worksheets.pdf
Pages 9 - 10

One *"Six Needs of Mourning"* game board worksheet

centerforloss.com
Worksheets.pdf
Page 11

"Six Needs of Mourning" game questions worksheet

centerforloss.com
Worksheets.pdf
Page 12

Index cards

Glue

One die

One game piece for each teen (try using pieces from Monopoly, Sorry, the Game of Life, or other games)

Copies of *"My Grief Rights: Ten Healing Rights for Grieving Teens"* worksheet

centerforloss.com
Worksheets.pdf
Page 13

Acknowledging the Death for Teens

SIX NEEDS OF MOURNING AND MY GRIEF RIGHTS

GOAL:

To introduce teens to the "six needs of mourning" as well as "My Grief Rights" to help them better understand the death of their loved ones and their rights in mourning

ACTIVITY:

1. Before the meeting, create the game board. You may want to decorate it a bit more and can add to it, if you wish. Print out the "Six Needs of Mourning" questions and glue each to an index card.

2. If this is the first meeting of the support group, allow each teen to share his or her story about the death of his or her loved one. Allow the teens the choice to pass.

3. Hand out copies of "Understanding Your Six Needs of Mourning for Teens" and explain each of the needs.

4. Play the Six Needs of Mourning game. Using one die and a game piece for each person, have the oldest person in the group begin.

5. After rolling the die, the player moves forward according to the number on the die.

6. Each time she lands, she must draw a card and try to answer it. Place the answered card on the bottom of the pile.

7. The person who has exactly the correct die number to reach the end is the winner.

8. Hand out "My Grief Rights: Ten Healing Rights for Grieving Teens." If time permits, go through this handout. If not, ask the teens to read it at home, letting them know that you will talk about this at the next session. (Wallet cards of "My Grief Rights" can be purchased from centerforloss.com/bookstore).

Autobiopoems of Myself and My Loved One

(The session before this one, ask each teen to bring in some objects and pictures that are about them and some that remind them of the person who died.)

Most teens accept the reality of the death on an intellectual level, understanding what happens physically when a person dies. Full acceptance on a "head" and "heart" level, though, can often take weeks or months.

GOAL:

To help teens move toward fully accepting the reality of the death on an emotional, or "heart," level

ACTIVITY:

1. Talk about the similarities and differences between each teen and the person who died.

2. Hand out and read "All is Well." Ask for comments.

3. Introduce autobiographical poems, or autobiopoems, and hand out the worksheets. You may want to have examples handy.

4. Explain that they are going to write two poems, one about themselves and one about the person who died.

5. Allow the teens time to complete the worksheets.

6. After they have finished, they should give the poems to you. Before the next session, type them into the format that is shown on the bottom of each sheet. Give the final copies to the teens at the next session so they can place them in the decorated frames created in step 7.

7. Hand out two 8.5" x 11" white frames to each teen. Give the teens time to decorate each of these with one representing themselves and the other representing the person who died. They can use some of the objects they brought or the materials you have.

8. If time remains, play The Game of Life.

AGE GROUP:

Teens

MATERIALS:

Copies of the poem, *"All is Well,"* worksheet

> centerforloss.com
> Worksheets.pdf
> Page 14

One copy of each Autobiopoem worksheet for each teen (one about themselves and one about their loved one)

> centerforloss.com
> Worksheets.pdf
> Pages 15 -16

Two 8.5" x 11" white frames for each teen

Decorative objects for each teen (consider beads, stickers, permanent markers)

Glue

The Game of Life

Teens

MATERIALS:

Copies of the *"Elephant in the Room"* poem, available from esdeer.com/elephant

Copies of the *"Questions About the Acknowledgment of the Death"* worksheet

centerforloss.com
Worksheets.pdf
Page 17

Large sheet of paper

Pens, pencils, and markers

Gray clay

The Elephant in the Room

Many teens have difficulties talking about the deaths. They pretend they are OK but may be really hurting inside.

GOAL:

To give teens a chance to talk about the deaths and express the ways in which they wish the people in their lives would acknowledge the deaths

ACTIVITY:

1. Talk about the definition of an "elephant in the room." (An elephant in the room is a problem that everyone knows very well but no one talks about because it is taboo, embarrassing, etc.)

2. Ask the teens if they have experienced this since the people they love died.

3. Brainstorm different types of elephants in the room, like death, prison, drugs or alcohol, abuse, etc.

4. Read the "Elephant in the Room" poem and discuss it.

5. Hand out the "Acknowledgment Questions" sheet to each of the teens. Give them about five to seven quiet minutes to complete this individually.

6. Using a large sheet of paper, write the same questions at the top and have the teens put their responses in the areas provided.

7. Discuss the remarks on the paper after each person has written his or her comments.

8. Using clay, have the teens actually make an elephant. They may actually want to use this when they feel there is an "elephant in the room."

The Obituary of My Loved One

When teens experience the death of someone loved, their world is often turned upside down, and they are now surrounded by pain and confusing emotions. Often, they do not get to say goodbye and have little to no involvement with the obituary and the funeral.

GOAL:
To help teens acknowledge the death through creating new, more meaningful obituaries for the people who died

ACTIVITY:
1. Talk with the teens about the obituaries that were written about their loved ones, as well as the funerals. Give each teen a chance to talk.

2. Explain that because of time and money, obituaries in the paper and online often do not do justice describing the lives of loved ones.

3. Tell the teens that tonight they will be given the chance to write a longer obituary, in their own words, about the lives of the people who died.

4. Using the "Writing an Obituary" worksheet, have the teens fill out the information that they know about the person who died.

5. Ask them to take this home and write up the information into a narrative.

6. If time remains, play The Game of Scattergories.

AGE GROUP:

Teens

MATERIALS:

Copies of the "*Writing an Obituary*" worksheet

centerforloss.com
Worksheets.pdf
Pages 18 - 20

The Game of Scattergories, available from Amazon

Embrace the pain of the loss

This need of mourning requires the children and teens to embrace the pain of their loss, which is sometimes very hard. It is easier to avoid, repress, or deny the pain of grief than it is to confront it, yet it is in confronting their pain that they will learn to reconcile themselves to it.

Children and teens will probably discover that they need to "dose" themselves in embracing their pain. In other words, they cannot (nor should they try to) overload themselves with the hurt all at one time. Sometimes they may need to distract themselves from the pain of the death, while at other times they will need to create a safe place to move toward it.

Unfortunately, our culture tends to encourage the denial of pain. If children and teens openly express their feelings of grief, misinformed friends and adults may advise them to "carry on" or "keep your chin up." If, on the other hand, they remain "strong" and "in control," they may be congratulated for "doing well" with their grief. But "doing well with their grief" actually means that they are becoming acquainted with their pain.

The activities in this section are designed to help children and teens express themselves emotionally, socially, cognitively, physically, and spiritually. These activities also encourage children and teens to ask questions, hear about the stories and expressions of other children and teens, and learn some coping skills.

Your companion in the second need of mourning is the cloudless sulphur. This butterfly reminds us that facing adversity is difficult but ultimately worth it if we want to get anywhere.

Remember to always think of the activity as the secondary task to accomplish for the group. The first task is to get the group members to express their grief and connect with each other. The game or activity is just a medium through which these tasks may be accomplished.

AGE GROUP:

Early Childhood

SESSION 1 MATERIALS:

I Miss You: A First Look at Death by Pat Thomas, available from Amazon

Roll of butcher paper, large enough to trace each child on

Scissors

Different colored construction paper

Yarn

Markers

Body Map

(Two-session lesson)

There are many feelings associated with grief. Young children can experience these feelings emotionally, mentally, physically, socially, and spiritually.

GOAL:

To help the children identify their feelings surrounding the deaths and give the adults in their lives a tool to understand how the children are feeling

SESSION 1 ACTIVITY:

1. Read aloud and discuss *I Miss You: A First Look at Death*.

2. Using the butcher paper, roll out a suitable length and trace the outline of each child's body. Cut each shape out.

3. Allow the children to decorate their paper bodies with colored paper for clothes, yarn for hair, and markers to draw faces.

4. Label each body with the name of the child and keep them for the next session.

SESSION 2 ACTIVITY:

1. Read aloud and discuss *I'll Always Love You.*

2. Talk especially about the feelings the boy has about the death of Elfie. Using the feelings below, talk about them as they relate to the death of a pet or someone loved.

3. Bring out the body cutouts from session one and distribute them to their makers.

SESSION 2 MATERIALS:

4. You can use the key below or devise your own system for indicating each feeling. Let the children tape the shapes on their cutout bodies where they have each feeling. For example, if a child stomps his feet when he is angry, suggest putting the starbursts on the feet. Do not insist on a particular feeling going in a certain place; each child will have his or her own feelings and feel them in different places.

   - Red starbursts – Anger (could be on feet)
   - Blue tears – Sadness (could be near eyes)
   - Yellow stars – Surprise or shock (could be near brain)
   - Green flowers – Guilt or "if onlys" (could be near the stomach)
   - Pink flowers – Love and hope (could be near the heart)
   - Band-Aids – Comfort, coping, support (could be near shoulders)

   Type up this key or your modified key and glue it on the back of each child's cutout body so that his or her parent or guardian understands the symbolism, too.

5. End the session by having the children explain "their body" to the other group members.

I'll Always Love You by Hans Wilhelm, available from Amazon

Shapes for the different feelings (See key to the left. Can use stickers for each shape or shapes can be created out of construction paper.)

Tape for sticking shapes to bodies

Early Childhood

MATERIALS:

The Feelings Book by Todd Parr, available from Amazon

Feelings Bingo, free download from SpeechTherapyGames. com or HubbardsCupboard.org. Alternately, you can create your own Feelings Bingo game.

Feeling Cards (use the calling cards from your bingo game)

Apple or other small object

How Do I Feel?

Young children do not understand the abstract concept of death, but they do have feelings. Children's feelings are their friends. Feelings help children pay better attention to their grief. Through this attention comes their own understanding about the death they are grieving.

GOAL:
To allow the children a place to talk about their feelings

ACTIVITY:
1. Talk about feelings. Highlight the specific feelings that will be included in your bingo game. As you say the emotion, give the children a chance to share when they felt this way.

2. Read aloud and discuss *The Feelings Book*.

3. Play Feelings Bingo.

4. If time permits, play this game like Hot Potato. Ask the children to sit in a circle and give one child an apple. When the music starts, have the children pass the apple around the circle. But when the music stops, the child who is holding the apple in his or her hand has to draw a feelings card (from the calling cards used for bingo) and act out the feeling on the card. The other children must guess what feeling is being displayed.

I'm Gonna Like Me Even When I'm Angry

Young children may believe a parent, grandparent, brother, or sister died because they had once wished the person dead when angry. They also have feelings about the death that most often are expressed through behavior (e.g. play, acting out). These feelings are normal.

GOAL:
To help the children identify good ways to cope with their anger

ACTIVITY:
1. Discuss the feelings that each of them have toward the death and ask them why they feel this way.

2. Let them know that today this group will be focusing on anger and how to deal with it.

3. Read *I'm Gonna Like Me*. After you've finished, ask why it is important to like themselves, even when they are angry or sad or frustrated.

4. Talk about anger and what happens when they are angry. Ask them what they do when they are angry. Also discuss the good and bad ways to handle their anger. Examples might be:

AGE GROUP:
Early Childhood

MATERIALS:

I'm Gonna Like Me: Letting Off a Little Self-Esteem by Jamie Lee Curtis, available from Amazon

Clay

Toothpicks

BAD WAYS:
- Break something
- Scream at someone
- Bite someone
- Be mean to a pet
- Throw a temper tantrum
- Hit somebody

GOOD WAYS:
- Hug a stuffed animal
- Have a good cry
- Draw a picture
- Rip up old newspapers
- Walk away from the situation

- Play with clay or water
- Bounce a ball
- Take deep, slow breaths
- Ask for help
- Go someplace quiet to cool down

5. Give a piece of clay to each child. Have them first just pound the clay, as this is a coping skill. Let them know this is something they can do when they get angry. Then they may make a face that either shows their anger or helps them cope with the anger.

Early Childhood

MATERIALS:

Large sheet of paper

Samantha Jane's Missing Smile by Julie Kaplow and Donna Pincus, available from Amazon

Various sizes of cotton balls or pompoms (tiny, small, and large)

Googly eyes

Yarn

Glue

Warm Fuzzies

The most basic feeling of loss for a child is that of fear. They may be uncertain about what happened and ask questions questions such as, Who will die next? How will we live without the dead person? Will my parents ever be happy again? Will my other parent die? How often does death happen? Who will take care of me? Where will I go if I die? Why did it happen to me? And, most especially, will *I* die?

GOAL:

To help children learn how to cope with the fear that comes after losing someone loved

ACTIVITY:

1. Talk with the children about their fears. As they say them, write them on the large sheet of paper.

2. Read aloud and discuss *Samantha Jane's Missing Smile.*

3. After reading this book, look back at the poster and see if any of the children's fears were brought up in the story.

4. Ask the children how they usually cope with their fears, especially the ones listed on the paper.

5. Explain that there are many ways to cope with fears. Some of these might be:

   • Talking with an adult or older sibling

   • Talking with their teacher

   • Finding a safe place to be

   • Breathing deep

   • Imagining a safe place in their minds

   • Hugging a pet

6. Explain that today they are going to make a "warm fuzzy" to hold when they are feeling scared.

7. Using three large cotton balls, glue them together to form what looks like the body of a snowman.

8. Glue googly eyes on the top cotton ball for a face.

9. Use two smaller cotton balls for the ears and one very small cotton ball for the nose. You can use different colors to create unique "warm fuzzies."

10. To form the smile, use a small piece of yarn.

11. The completed project should look something like this:

12. Ask the children to let you know at the next session if and when they used their "warm fuzzies."

MATERIALS:

Large sheet of paper

Sometimes I am Bombaloo by Rachel Vail, available from Amazon

Different colored beads, one color for each emotion

Elastic string

Scissors

Expression Beads

It is important to give children an outlet to share their grief experiences and express their feelings, concerns, and fears. The process of expressing or diffusing these feelings can be helpful for several reasons:

- Expressing fears or concerns can relieve tension or anxiety.

- Telling and retelling their stories helps children create a sense of order, coherence, or control over events that seem chaotic, confusing, or overwhelming.

- Hearing other children's stories helps them realize that they are not alone in their fears or concerns.

- The interactions between children and adults, or among children, that come with the sharing or experiences or feelings can build a sense of security and trust.

- Expressing feelings helps children organize and sort through how they feel about death, dying, and their own loss.

GOAL:
To let the children express the different feelings they have

ACTIVITY:
1. Ask the children what feelings they are experiencing as a result of the death. As they respond, write these answers on a large sheet of paper.

2. Read aloud and discuss *Sometimes I am Bombaloo.*

3. Looking at the list of feelings that the children generated earlier, see if there are any other feelings that they want to add to the list now. Then try to put them in categories such as: sad, mad, frustrated, scared, confused, lonely, guilty,

and nervous. You can have as many categories of emotions as you have colors of beads.

4. Using the beads, agree on what colors are going to represent each of the above feelings. For example, red could stand for sadness, black for madness or anger, etc.

5. Using elastic string, allow the children to make one necklace and one bracelet.

6. If possible, have a volunteer make a key for each child so they are reminded of which color represents which feeling.

7. Talk about how they can use these bracelets alone and when with others.

AGE GROUP:

Elementary

MATERIALS:

Index cards

Is a Worry Worrying You? by Ferida Wolff, available from Amazon

Craft sticks

Yarn in several different colors

Small buttons or googly eyes

Tacky glue

Guatemalan Worry Dolls

(This activity may take two sessions.)

After a death of a loved one, children often worry. Children may already worry about what they will wear to school, the grade they will get on a test, if someone will like them, or if they will make the baseball team. But after someone loved has died, they may worry about who will take care of them or whether other people they love will die. They may even worry that they are going to die.

Worry dolls are small yarn or string dolls that were first made in Guatemala. Each night before children went to sleep, they would tell the dolls their worries and place them under their pillows. During the night, the dolls would worry in place of the children, so the children could sleep untroubled and wake up without their worries.

GOAL:
To help the children find ways to let go of their worries

ACTIVITY:

1. Beginning with one of the children, encourage him or her to share things that he or she worries about. It does not have to be related to the death. List each thing separately on the front of an index card. On the back of the card, write down suggestions from the group for how to counteract that worry. For example, one worry might be getting picked on during the bus ride to school. Strategies to deal with this worry might include telling adults such as a teacher or the bus driver, or sitting with friends. Do this for each child. Once you believe most of his or her worries are represented, continue with the next child. Remind each of them to get into the habit of actively referring to these cards when problems come up. (This part of the activity may take one session.)

2. Read and discuss *Is a Worry Worrying You?*

3. Explain to the kids what Guatemalan worry dolls are. You can use the description above or do a little of your own online research.

4. Have the children glue two craft sticks together to form a person-like cross. Wrap yarn around the dolls for clothes and hair and glue in place. Use buttons or googly eyes for the eyes.

5. If time remains, the children may make another doll.

Elementary

MATERIALS:

One mirror for each child, or one mirror to pass around

Copies of the *"My Mirror Image"* worksheet

centerforloss.com
Worksheets.pdf
Page 21

Colored pencils, crayons, and markers

Connie's Many Feelings board game, available from Amazon

Mirror, Mirror on the Wall

By looking at a child, it is often difficult to gauge what he or she is feeling inside. Because children grieve in doses, a child may at one moment be sad and the next expressing joy. Sometimes children are upset but they may not be able to articulate why. Giving them the time and encouragement to share their feelings, as well as encouraging the development of coping skills, may enable them to sort out their many feelings.

GOAL:

To help the children express the feelings they are having inside that other people may not see

ACTIVITY:

1. Talk about the feelings the children are having after the deaths of their loved ones. Are their feelings different in different places? For example, at home, at school, with friends, at church, or with other family members?

2. Give each child a mirror and ask what he or she sees in the mirror. Alternately, pass around one mirror and ask each child in turn. Aim for a consensus of "physical appearance," but accept other options.

3. Ask the children what cannot be seen in a mirror. Aim for "feelings inside."

4. Using the "My Mirror Image" worksheet, have the children draw their physical pictures.

5. Have them list their feelings about the death on the other side of the worksheet, since feelings are not always shown on the outside.

6. If time remains, play the game Connie's Many Feelings.

Take A Deep Breath

Coping skills are effective in helping children deal with the death of someone loved. Deep belly breathing, known as diaphragmatic breathing, helps children learn how to become calm and has a positive impact on children's health and immune systems. It can lower stress and anxiety levels. It can be used to decrease pain and anger. Breathing can also be used anytime, anywhere.

GOAL:
To introduce the children to breathing as a coping technique

ACTIVITY:

1. Ask the children what techniques they use when they are stressed or angry.

2. Read the book *A Boy and a Bear: The Children's Relaxation Book*.

3. Discuss the proper mechanics of breathing and how the children can use it to calm down when they are angry, stressed, or afraid. Have the kids lie on the floor. They should put their hands on their stomachs and feel the stomach go out when they inhale through their noses and come in when they exhale. Have them practice this for a few minutes. You might want to include peaceful music to reduce distractions and help them concentrate on their breathing.

4. Using their deep breathing skills, play Ping-Pong Phooey (see directions on page 30).

5. If time permits, play with the coping skills cards from The Good Mourning Game. These cards introduce techniques that can help children work through the grieving process. The children will learn to share memories, explore feelings, enjoy laughter and play, relax, and identify their own coping strategies.

AGE GROUP:

Elementary

MATERIALS:

A Boy and a Bear: The Children's Relaxation Book by Lori Light, available from Amazon

Six Ping-Pong balls

Folding table the children can kneel or stand around

Coping skills cards from The Good Mourning Game, available from CreativeTherapyStore. com, or you can search childhoodinterventions. blogspot.com for "coping skills flash-cards" to get an idea of how you can make your own

SUPPLIES:

Six Ping-Pong balls

Table

PING-PONG PHOOEY DIRECTIONS

1. Have participants gather around the table on their knees.

2. Ask if any of them have played Ping-Pong before. Explain that they are going to play a game of group Ping-Pong...without using paddles or hands. Ask if they have any ideas about what else they can use to move the Ping-Pong ball around.

3. Explain that they are going to use only their breath to pass the Ping-Pong ball around, using the deep breathing techniques they just practiced. The goal is to not let the Ping-Pong ball fall off the table as they pass it to each other. Passing the ball doesn't have to occur in a circle; it can be random.

4. As the participants get familiar with the activity, add another Ping-Pong ball into the game. Keep on gradually adding additional Ping-Pong balls until all six are in play.

Grief Response Cards

It is important for teens to know that there are universal common grief responses. Knowing and understanding these grief reactions helps to normalize their personal experience and diminish distress as a result of the intensity of the grief. When teens know and understand common grief responses, and have others in their lives who know and understand, this becomes a supportive validation of their personal grief responses.

GOAL:
To help teens realize that many of their feelings are normal and felt by others too

ACTIVITY:
1. Pass out copies of the "Common Teen Responses to Grief" worksheet. A copy is also included on pages 32-33 for your reference. Review with the teens some of the common reactions of grief. Take some time to read all the way through this sheet.

2. Stack the grief response cards face down according to color. Group members take turns tossing a die. They then draw the top card of the color on the die. (If using a regular die, each color will correspond to a number.) Have the teens share the reaction with the group and say whether or not they have experienced it in their grief journey.

3. Keep a tally of the various responses on a large sheet of paper where everyone can see. When all the cards have been drawn, you can refer back to the tally marks to reinforce how common these reactions are.

4. Remind the group that these reactions are normal and will change over time.

5. If time remains, play the game On the Road to Discovery.

AGE GROUP:

Teens

MATERIALS:

Copies of the *"Common Teen Responses to Grief"* worksheet

 centerforloss.com
Worksheets.pdf
Page 22

Copies of the Grief Response Cards

centerforloss.com
Worksheets.pdf
Page 23 - 36

Large sheet of paper

A die with different colors on each face (a regular die can be substituted if needed)

On the Road To Discovery game, available from ADDWarehouse.com

COMMON TEEN RESPONSES TO GRIEF

People often think of grief as an emotional experience. It is. Grief is also a physical, emotional, behavioral, and spiritual experience. It not only affects how a person feels but also how a person behaves. Here are some common ways teens respond to grief:

PHYSICAL RESPONSES

Deep sighing

Weakness and fatigue

Rapid heartbeat

Increased blood pressure

Increase in activity

Decrease in activity

Muscular tension

Sleep disturbances

Decreased resistance to illness

Change in weight and appetite

Neglect of self

Increased sensory awareness

Increase in self-care

EMOTIONAL RESPONSES

Numbness

Confusion

Sadness

Guilt

Euphoria

Yearning

Despair

Hopelessness

Helplessness

Feeling of being lost

Anger

Bitterness/vengefulness

Peacefulness

Spiritual connectedness

BEHAVIORAL RESPONSES

Searching for what was lost

Detaching from surroundings

Disoriented to time and place

Withdrawn from friends and activities

Unable to concentrate

Forgetful

Blameful of others

Apathetic regarding activities or future

Preoccupied

Crying

Seeking solitude

Finishing "unfinished business"

Seeking and providing forgiveness

Spontaneity

SOCIAL RESPONSES

Acting or tying to be like the person who died

Missing school a lot

Not wanting to leave home

Taking care of other people too much

Inability to talk about the death

Acting older than other kids in age group

SOCIAL RESPONSES
(continued)

Stealing things from others

Fighting with friends or other family members

Doing things that are high risk and could be dangerous

Feeling different from peers

SPIRITUAL RESPONSES

Searching for what was lost

Loss of faith

Renewal of faith

Feeling punished for some wrong

Anger at God

Helplessness

Confusion

Comforted by spiritual beliefs

Hopelessness

Insecurity

WARNING SIGNS

Destructive behavior

Compulsive caregiving

Taking on too much responsibility

A sustained drop in school performance

Independence beyond one's years

Stealing

Depression

Substance abuse

Early sexual activity or promiscuity

Getting stuck at an early developmental stage

Difficulty in relationships

School phobia

Increased fighting and aggression

Eating disorders

High risk-taking

Inability to talk about the loss of the person who died

Over-identification with the death of the person who died

MATERIALS:

Copies of *"Common Coping Skills for Teens After the Death of Someone Loved"* worksheet

centerforloss.com
Worksheets.pdf
Page 37 - 39

Highlighters

Several colors of clay

Sample images of joy, peace, calm

How to Cope with My Feelings

When coping with a death, teens may go through all kinds of emotions. They may be sad, worried, or scared. They might be shocked, unprepared, or confused. They might be feeling angry, cheated, relieved, guilty, exhausted, or just plain empty. Their emotions might be stronger or deeper than usual or mixed together in ways they have never experienced before. Some teens find they have trouble concentrating, studying, sleeping, or eating when they're coping with a death. Others lose interest in activities they used to enjoy. Some teens lose themselves in playing computer games or eat or drink to excess. And some feel numb, as if nothing has happened. All of these are normal ways to react to a death.

GOAL:

To help teens develop ways to cope with their various feelings after the deaths

ACTIVITY:

1. Talk about the feelings that the teens are currently experiencing as a result of the death. Engage them in a discussion about how they are coping with these emotions.

2. Hand out the "Common Coping Skills for Teens" worksheet.

3. Give the teens some time to look through these.

4. Ask them to highlight five coping skills that they are either using or would like to use. There is room at the bottom for each teen to add more coping skills if they wish.

5. If they want, the teens can share a new coping skill they want to try with the rest of the group.

6. Let the teens know they'll be playing with clay today, number 24 on their list.

7. Using different colors of clay, the teens will make objects that to them symbolize something joyful or being calm or at peace. These images may remind them of the person who died but are intended for use as objects that bring calmness, peace, and joy to their lives. You can print out different images, such as flowers, butterflies, and sunrises, from the internet to give them a starting point.

NEED #2: EMBRACE THE PAIN OF THE LOSS

Show and Hide Feelings

Many teens have difficulties expressing their emotions after someone dies. Teens grieve, whether or not another person can see it. Like adults, a teen experiences a broad range of emotions and physical reactions. But teens often grieve differently than adults. For example, the death of a close teen friend may evoke more intense grief than the death of a grandparent. Adults who don't expect this may minimize the impact of the death of a peer because they don't acknowledge or understand the significance of this friendship to the teen.

GOAL:

To allow teens a way to identify those feelings and emotions they share with the world and those they keep hidden or secret

ACTIVITY:

1. Discuss with the teens the myriad emotions and physical reactions they have had since the death of their loved ones.

2. Hand out one lunch-size paper bag to each teen.

3. The outside of the bag should be decorated with their names, and words, symbols, and pictures that describe them.

4. On index cards, have the teens write down topics or issues they have struggled with since the death as well as feelings they have kept inside. These will be placed inside the paper bag.

5. When they are done, have the teens share some of the characteristics that describe them, as well as one or two issues that they are struggling with or feelings they haven't shared with anyone.

6. Let them know that you will keep the bags until the end of the support group, at which time they will be returned so the teens can see the progress they have made.

7. If time permits, play the Bridge of Self-Confidence Game for Teens.

AGE GROUP:

Teens

MATERIALS:

One lunch-size paper bag for each teen

Index cards

Markers

Bridge of Self-Confidence Game for Teens, available from SelfHelp-Warehouse.com

MATERIALS:

Copies of the *"Checklist of Emotions"* worksheet

centerforloss.com
Worksheets.pdf
Pages 40 - 42

Pens and pencils

Marble racing game (check Amazon or your local toy store for affordable kits)

Two decks of old cards

Copies of the *"Prepare Your Response Plan for Grief Triggers"* worksheet

centerforloss.com
Worksheets.pdf
Pages 43 - 44

Ker Plunk

Dominoes

Triggers

(This activity may take two peer support sessions because it is important for teens to understand the concept of triggers.)

When experiencing the death of a loved one, teens often experience many emotions as they embrace their pain. Triggers are acts that set some course of events in motion. Both happy and sad memories have their triggers. The role of the mind in healing is extremely powerful and at other times extremely limiting. But grief triggers are to be expected. That's the way memory works. It is important to try and allow the memory to unfold with heartfelt pain so that it moves through and out of the teen.

GOAL:

To help the teens understand the role triggers play in their journey through grief

ACTIVITY:

1. Define triggers for the teens. A trigger is an act that sets some course of events in motion. For example, a green light causes cars on a road to move forward after being stopped. Or, your stomach growls so you get up and walk over to the refrigerator and grab a snack. Ask the teens for more real life examples of triggers.

2. Explain that they are going to do some fun activities that involve triggers. But before they do, they will each fill out the "Checklist of Emotions" worksheet. Allow the teens enough time to complete the worksheet.

3. Depending on the size of the group, have one or two trigger activities going on. One activity would be the marble racing game and the other would be a game of card stacking. If you're only playing one game, let the teens decide which they'd prefer.

4. Have the teens draw some conclusions about triggers. For example, sometimes just one card

slipping can cause the entire structure to collapse; small events can cause wider ripples.

5. Talk about triggers related to death. These could be things like a familiar smell or the sight of a piece of clothing. Places, people, and objects can also trigger memories of the person who died. What sort of triggers have the teens experienced? How did they feel?

6. Share some of your own stories about grief triggers and what you have experienced. Let the teens know that feeling sadness, loneliness, anger, anxiety, a lack of interest, or trouble sleeping or eating are all absolutely normal emotions to feel when grief has been triggered.

7. Talk about how the teens can respond when grief triggers occur and have them fill in the "Response Plan" worksheet.

8. End with playing Ker Plunk or dominoes, whichever the teens prefer.

Remember the person who died

When someone loved dies, children and teens have a continued relationship with this person based on their memories. Precious memories, dreams reflecting the significance of the relationship, and objects that link the child or teen to the person who died (such as photos, souvenirs etc.) are examples of some of the things that give testimony to a different form of a continued relationship. This need of mourning allows and encourages the children and teens to pursue this relationship.

But some people may try to take their memories away. Trying to be helpful, they encourage the children and teens to take down all the photos of the people who died. They tell them to keep busy or even to try to forget the people who died. But remembering the past allows children and teens to hope for the future. Their future will become open to new experiences only to the extent that they embrace the past.

The activities in this section are designed to help the children and teens remember different aspects of the people who died, share their memories, and celebrate the lives of the people who died. To help the children and teens have a continued relationship with the people who died, some activities will show them how they have similar traits to the people who died and others will find out what senses evoke memories of the people who died.

Your companion through the third need of mourning is the monarch butterfly. The monarch is the most commonly known butterfly in North America and one of the most widely photographed. It reminds us to embrace the memories of the past and treasure the keepsakes we have after someone loved dies.

Remember to always think of the activity as the secondary task to accomplish for the group. The first task is to get the group members to express their grief and connect with each other. The game or activity is just a medium through which these tasks may be accomplished.

AGE GROUP:

Early Childhood

MATERIALS:

Memory objects

The Memory Box by Kirsten McLaughlin, available from the Centering Corporation

Small white cardboard boxes (try your local craft store)

Markers

Decorative objects, such as stickers, beads, gems, etc.

Glue

Paper for notes

Memory Boxes

(The session before this one, ask each child to bring in some objects and pictures that remind him or her of the person who died.)

There are many great activities that help young children process the death of someone loved, but building a memory box with grieving children can be therapeutic for everyone involved. Grieving children need positive activities that will allow them to express their grief and fear in a fun, and therefore safe, way. Memory boxes encourage the discussion of memories and become a treasure for the future.

GOAL:

To give the children a concrete place for their positive memories

ACTIVITY:

1. Have the children talk with each other about the memory objects that they each brought in. Ask them questions about each of these objects, especially asking why they chose these objects and the significance that each of them have.

2. Read aloud and discuss *The Memory Box.*

3. Let each child decorate a white cardboard box with markers and other objects. Encourage the children to draw memories about the person who died or pictures of the family before the death.

4. Have the children place the memory objects they brought inside the now-decorated boxes.

5. Encourage them to add little notes and drawings too. Anything they want to put in the box is fine. Again, encourage discussion about each object. This is a safe and gentle way to dig into the conversation about the death.

6. Remind them to keep their boxes in a safe place and encourage them to add more memories as they think of them.

7. These memory boxes can be used when the children really miss the people who died.

Memory Frames

(The session before this one, ask each child to bring in pictures and small objects that remind him or her of the person who died. These will be glued onto a frame.)

Memories and dreams reflect the significance of the relationship between the child and the person who died. Linking objects, like photos and souvenirs, help the child convert the relationship with the person who died from one of presence to one of memory.

GOAL:
To create another way of keeping the children's memories alive

ACTIVITY:
1. Talk about the word "memory" and what it means. Ask the children if they remember anything from when they were three years old. What about four years old? Five years old?

2. What memories do they have of the person who died?

3. Read aloud and discuss *Sweet, Sweet Memories*.

4. Hand out the frames.

5. Have each child choose a piece of colored construction paper. Glue this to the back of the frame.

6. Then they may decorate the frame with objects, letters, and words that remind them of the person they are missing.

7. When the children are done, have them share these frames with each other, talking about some of the memories they have on the frames.

8. These frames are great to keep at your meeting place for use in other memory activities and at times of sadness.

9. If you do keep the frames with you, don't forget to allow the children to take them home when their time with the group is over.

AGE GROUP:
Early Childhood

MATERIALS:

Sweet, Sweet Memories by Jacqueline Woodson, available from Amazon

White 8.5" x 11" white matte frames. You may also create your own frames out of white foam board.

Colored construction paper

Glue sticks

Scissors

Stickers, gems, and other items for decorations

MATERIALS:

Wilfrid Gordon McDonald Partridge by Mem Fox, available from Amazon

CD player or iPod speakers

Melissa & Doug Band in a Box (contains six instruments), available from Amazon. You may also wish to create instruments out of materials handy, such as beans in a paper cup for a shaker. Your local music store may have cheap maracas and tambourines.

Music of choice

Never Gone

(The session before this one, ask each child to bring in a CD or iPod containing a piece of music that reminds him or her of the person who died. You may wish to ask the children's guardians to help.)

Memories of someone loved who has died are precious and important. Memories are meant to be shared with family. They trigger happiness and sadness, so it is all right to laugh and cry. Memories are something that will always be a part of you.

GOAL:
To use music as a way of remembering the people who died

ACTIVITY:

1. Have each child share two memories of their loved one.

2. Read aloud and discuss *Wilfrid Gordon McDonald Partridge*.

3. Discuss the different types of memories each of the older people in the book had.

4. Ask each child what music they each brought in.

5. Depending on the size of the group, listen to a portion or the entire piece of music that each child brought in. At the end of each piece of music, ask the child who brought it in how the piece makes him or her feel.

6. Using the Melissa & Doug Band in a Box, give each child an instrument. If you have more than six children, you may have to purchase an additional set or encourage the children to share.

7. Playing a CD of choice, have the children shake their instruments in time with the music.

8. Ask them what they think about how music and memories can interact.

Something Small

Celebrating the life of someone loved and his or her important place in the family will help in continuing traditions and keeping memories alive.

GOAL:
To help the children remember the special traditions they had with the people who died

ACTIVITY:
1. Talk about the special times and events the children remember that took place with the people who died. Ask each child how he or she felt during these times. Which activities does he want to keep? Are there any new activities that she has begun?

2. Read aloud and discuss *Something Small*. (Instead of printing the book, you may instead want to bring it up on a laptop.)

3. Using the "My Favorite Little Memories" worksheets, have the children draw pictures below the words. If they do not have a memory about this concept, either skip it or create a different concept.

4. When everyone is done, have each child share his or her little memories.

5. If time remains, play the game I Never Forget a Face.

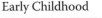

AGE GROUP:

Early Childhood

MATERIALS:

Something Small, a Sesame Street book, printable from sesamestreet.org

Copies of "*My Favorite Little Memories*" worksheet

centerforloss.com
Worksheets.pdf
Page 45

Crayons and markers

I Never Forget a Face game, available from Amazon

Elementary

MATERIALS:

Copies of the lyrics of "About Memories" by Mattie J. Stepanek and sung by Billy Gilman, available online through a Google search

CD player or laptop computer

Copies of *"A List of Possible Gifts"* worksheet

centerforloss.com
Worksheets.pdf
Page 46

One gift box per child, available from Paper-mart.com or your local craft store

Index cards cut in half

Markers

Glue sticks

Stickers

Other decorations (gems, ribbon, etc.)

One bow per child

About Memories

Memories reflect the significance of the relationship of the person who died. These memories allow children to have a continued relationship with that person. This need of mourning involves allowing and encouraging children to pursue this relationship.

GOAL:

To help the children create a safe place to keep their memories of the people who died

ACTIVITY:

1. Discuss the idea of memories and what a memory is. Memories are the brain's way of keeping and recalling past experiences. Not all memories are happy.

2. Hand out and read aloud the poem "About Memories" by Mattie Stepanek. Draw attention to the last lines: "Memories are a gift of the past / that we hold in the present. / To create what can be a great future / treasure and keep memories."

3. If you have the CD "Music Through Heartsongs" by Billy Gilman, play the track "About Memories." The song is also available on YouTube.

4. Explain to the children that tonight they are going to focus on memories of the person who died, along with memories that they are currently creating about themselves. Remind them that who they are, how they act, and what they think right now is actually a process of creating memories. In fact, they are creating gifts for themselves and others by working on different aspects of themselves.

5. Discuss "gifts" in the sense of non-material objects. Give the kids some examples from the "Possible Gifts" sheet. Have a few copies of the sheet around to show the kids if they want to copy from it.

6. Give each child a blank gift box. On the outside of the box, the children should write or draw the gifts that they are already giving to other people, especially their family.

7. On the inside of the box, the kids should write notes to the person who died. The focus of the note should be on telling the person who died what memories the children miss now that he or she is gone.

8. The outside of the box can be decorated more using markers, stickers, and other decorations.

9. When the kids are done, they may choose one bow and stick it on the outside.

10. Help the children understand that every time they want to remember their loved one, all they have to do is look in the box. They should be encouraged to add other memories as they remember them.

AGE GROUP:

Elementary

MATERIALS:

"Remember Me" poem, available on PoeticExpressions.co.uk (search "remember me")

Plain white placemats for each child or a large, thick piece of white paper

Fabric paints and markers in several colors

Tarps or newspaper

Decorative objects, like stickers, gems, feathers, pompoms, etc.

Hot glue

Memory objects

Lineup game, available from Amazon

Memory Mats

(The session before this one, ask each child to bring in some objects and pictures that remind him or her of the person who died.)

When someone loved has died, the memories of this person are very important to a child. These memories allow children to have a continued relationship with that person as they journey through grief.

GOAL:

To help the children create a place to keep some of their memories about the people who died

ACTIVITY:

1. Talk about the importance of having memories of the people who died. Encourage the children to talk about some of their favorite memories.

2. Read and discuss "Remember Me."

3. Distribute a plain white placemat to each child.

4. Children may place their pictures and objects on the mat for gluing. Glue the items down for them and put the placemats aside to dry before the children take them home.

5. If time remains, play the game Lineup.

Memory Quilts

(The session before this one, ask each child to bring in memory items of the person who died. You will need volunteers before and during this session for this activity.)

Memories of loved ones are worth preserving. A memory quilt is a collage of memory items and drawings that, when put together, helps trigger all sorts of pleasing memories and associations.

GOAL:
To create memory quilts for the children so they can treasure their memories for years to come

ACTIVITY:
1. Using samples of quilts, talk about what a quilt is.

2. Read aloud and discuss *The Patchwork Quilt* .

3. Using the Alex Toys Knot-A-Quilt kit, give each child nine squares. (The kit comes with 48 squares. One kit will have enough for five kids if each quilt is made with nine squares.)

4. Attach the squares by tying knots. (Instructions come in the box.)

5. Place the memory objects or drawings on the quilt and attach with tacky glue. This is where you will need the help of volunteers.

6. When the quilts are completed, have each child share his or her memory quilt with the group.

7. Allow the children to take the quilts home when the glue is dry.

AGE GROUP:

Elementary

MATERIALS:

Quilt samples; you can bring these from your home or have your volunteers bring some from theirs

The Patchwork Quilt by Valerie Flourney, available from Scholastic.com

Alex Toys Knot-A-Quilt kit, available from Amazon

Markers

Paper for drawings

Tacky glue

MATERIALS:

Sweet, Sweet Memories by Jacqueline Woodson, available from Amazon

Five rocks for each child, available from CuriousCountryCreations.com

Metallic markers

Watercolor paints and brushes

A glass or plastic container for each child's rocks; try Tupperware

One battery-operated tea light for each child

Memory Stones

When someone loved dies, children cherish their memories of this person. Remembering the past often makes the future hopeful. These memories will manifest themselves in dreams, memory books, photographs, stories, music, and many other areas. As children embrace the past, they become open to new experiences and relationships.

GOAL:

To help the children create a way to keep some of their most favorite memories

ACTIVITY:

1. Ask the children what some of their favorite memories are.

2. Read aloud and discuss *Sweet, Sweet Memories*.

3. Help each child write down five memories that they have of their loved one. These should be represented by one or two words, like "Ball games" or "Bedtime" or "Hugs."

4. These words can be written, using metallic markers, on five rocks.

5. Once the words are written, the children may paint their rocks using watercolor paint.

6. These rocks may be placed in a clear glass or plastic container, with a battery-operated tea light placed in it to illuminate their memories.

Fifty Ways to Remember

(The session before this one, ask the teens to bring pictures, objects, and any other mementos of their loved one, including music.)

Memories are one of the best legacies that exist after the death of someone loved. Teens will always remember. Instead of teens ignoring these memories, they need to share these with their family and friends. Memories can be tinged with both happiness and sadness. If memories bring laughter, smile. If the memories bring sadness, then it's all right to cry.

GOAL:
To help the teens create a memory box and learn more ways they can continue to remember the people who died

ACTIVITY:
1. Talk with the teens about their memories of the people who died. Encourage a sharing of these memories with the group.

2. Hand out a copy of "Fifty Ways To Remember" to each teen and give them time to read through the sheet.

3. Discuss some of these suggestions. Are they already making use of some of these? Are there others they might like to do?

4. Let the teens decorate the outside of their gift boxes.

5. Put any photographs in plastic covers to prevent them being damaged. Have the teens place the mementos they brought into their decorated memory boxes.

6. Encourage the teens to talk about some of the memories they now have stored in their memory boxes.

AGE GROUP:
Teens

MATERIALS:
Copies of the *"Fifty Ways to Remember"* worksheet

 centerforloss.com
Worksheets.pdf
Pages 47 - 48

One white gift box for each teen, available from Papermart.com or your local craft store

Decorating supplies such as paper, markers, and stickers

Photo covers

Scissors

Glue

MATERIALS:

Copies of the *"Letter To"* and *"Letter From"* worksheets

centerforloss.com
Worksheets.pdf
Pages 49 - 50

Pencils and pens

Apples to Apples, available from Amazon

Continuing the Dialogue

When someone loved dies, teens cherish their memories of this person. Remembering the past often makes the future hopeful. Memories, dreams reflecting the importance of the relationship, and objects that link a teen to their loved one are examples of some things that give testimony to a different form of a continued relationship. As teens embrace the past, they become open to new experiences and relationships.

GOAL:

To help the teens write letters to remember the people who died

ACTIVITY:

1. Talk about some of the memories that each teen has of the person who died. Encourage them to tell more than one.

2. Explain that they will be writing two letters today, one to the person who died and one from the person who died. Hand out a copy of each letter form to the teens.

3. Have the teens begin by picturing themselves with the person who died. If they know what they want to write about, let them go ahead. If they don't know what to write about, suggest one or two of the following:

   • Recall a funny thing that happened when you were together.

   • Remember some of the favorite things that you liked to do together.

   • Let the person who died know that you miss them, especially when...

   • Let the person who died know how and why you feel connected to him or her.

   • Bring the person who died up to speed on recent events, accomplishments, and feelings.

4. Then have the teens write a letter back from the people who died as they feel the people may respond.

5. If time remains, play the game Apples to Apples.

Music Memories

(At the session before this one, ask the teens to bring in the printed lyrics and music for their loved ones' favorite songs. They may bring in more than one song.)

Most grieving teens create safe places in their hearts for the memories of someone loved. Often, the five senses will bring back memories they may have forgotten about. Music is an ideal intervention for allowing teens to express feelings of grief because words are sometimes not enough.

GOAL:
To use music to help the teens remember the people who died

ACTIVITY:
1. Talk with the teens about what effects music has on their lives. Have them give examples of different kinds of effects.

2. The average person's heart rate is between 70-90 beats per minute (bpm), so music that is slower and between 60-80 bpm is the best choice when using it to calm and heal. Music billed as ambient, spiritual, or celestial will usually be at "heart-level" bpm or below.

3. Let them share the music they brought in; allow each teen to share as much or as little of the song or songs as they are comfortable with. Ask them how they feel when they hear a favorite song of the people who died.

4. Have them glue the lyrics of the song or songs they brought to a piece of construction paper.

5. They may decorate around the lyrics.

6. If time remains, play Glee Yahtzee.

AGE GROUP:
Teens

MATERIALS:
CD player or iPod speakers

9" x 12" colored construction paper

Glue

Markers, crayons, stickers, etc. for decorating

Glee Yahtzee, available from Amazon

MATERIALS:

Jenga game, available from Amazon

Questions from the *"Jenga Questions"* worksheet written on half the pieces (you may print out slips of paper and glue or tape them to the blocks if you don't wish to write on the game)

centerforloss.com
Worksheets.pdf
Page 51

Deck of cards (use more than one if the group is large)

Using Jenga to Build Memories

A relationship of memory is a special kind of relationship for teens who are experiencing the death of someone loved. Teens use things like memory boxes, photos, and linking objects as a testimony to a different form of continued relationship with the person who died. Allowing and encouraging the teen to pursue this relationship will help them on their journey toward healing.

GOAL:

To help the teens express memories of the people who died

ACTIVITY:

1. Talk about the memories that the teens have of the people who died. Don't focus only on the good memories, but bring up some bad ones as well.

2. Explain that "Jenga" comes from a Swahili word meaning to build.

3. Remind the teens of the rules of Jenga and tell them of the new rule: When a teen removes a block with a question on it, he or she must answer that question. Others may answer too after the teen who drew the block is finished. Out of the 54 pieces in Jenga, 27 will have questions.

4. If time remains, have the teens play the Memory Concentration Game. The goal is to collect the most pairs of cards.

5. Shuffle the cards and lay them face down on the table in a rectangle. The youngest player goes first. Play then proceeds clockwise.

6. On each turn, a player turns over two cards (one at a time) and keeps them if they match numbers. If a successful match is made, that player also gets to take another turn.

7. When a player turns over two cards that do not match numbers, those cards are turned face down again and it becomes the next player's turn.

8. The game is over when all the pairs have been removed.

Develop a new self-identity

Part of self-identity comes from the relationships children and teens have with other people. When someone loved dies, they must begin the difficult process of forming an identity apart from that person.

A death often requires children and teens to take on new roles that had been filled by the people who died. Examples of these are performing chores they usually didn't before or babysitting younger siblings. Every time they do something that used to be done by the people who died, their identities are questioned. They may feel a temporarily heightened dependence on others as well as feelings of helplessness, frustration, inadequacy, and fear.

Some children and teens discover some positive aspects of their changed self-identity. They may develop a renewed confidence in themselves, or they may develop a more caring, kind, and sensitive part of themselves.

The activities in this section are designed to help children and teens focus on their positive traits; adapt to changes; become aware of their physical, emotional, social, cognitive, and spiritual growth; look to the future; become invested in their "new life"; and create a vision and mission for themselves.

In the fourth need of mourning, the pipevine swallowtail butterfly is your companion. Just as butterflies transform from caterpillars to the colorful, flying bugs we all recognize, grieving children and teens are changed when someone loved dies. It is your job to help them discover who they are now.

Remember to always think of the activity as the secondary task to accomplish for the group. The first task is to get the group members to express their grief and connect with each other. The game or activity is just a medium through which these tasks may be accomplished.

MATERIALS:

I Feel Orange Today
by Patricia Godwin,
available from Barnes
& Noble

Six paper hearts for
each child

centerforloss.com
Worksheets.pdf
Page 52

Labels for hearts

Glue

Markers and crayons

Sturdy paper plates

Celebrating Me

When young children experience a death, their self-identity or the way they see themselves can change. A death often requires the children to take on new roles that had been filled by the people who died. Therefore, it is important for these young children to focus on their positive aspects.

GOAL:

To help the children learn who they are and how they feel about different things

ACTIVITY:

1. Ahead of time, print copies of the heart templates. Each child will need six hearts, each of a different color. I recommend printing on colored paper to save ink. Also before the session, print copies of the mood labels found in step 7 of the instructions.

2. Describe a mood as the way someone feels at a particular time. There are different moods for different events.

3. Ask them questions like

   • What mood are you in when it is your birthday?

   • What mood are you in when a friend gets hurt?

   • What mood are you in when someone yells at you?

   • What mood are you in when you watch a scary movie?

4. Read aloud and discuss *I Feel Orange Today*. (If you wish, you can purchase a copy of the book for each child to have and take home, but this is not necessary.)

5. Ask the children to describe the mood they are currently experiencing or a mood that they experienced earlier that day (or last night, yesterday, etc.). Do these moods have colors?

6. Pass out the six hearts and mood labels to each child.

7. Have the children attach one of the following mood labels to each heart.

    * I feel happy when...
    * I feel scared when...
    * I feel sad when...
    * I feel mad when...
    * I feel hurt when...
    * I feel proud when...

8. If they can complete the sentence themselves, then allow them to do so. Otherwise, please write down their thoughts.

9. If they wish, the children can draw pictures on their hearts to help illustrate the moods.

10. Cut out the center of each paper plate. On the edge of the plates, glue each child's six hearts. Allow them to take these wreaths home.

10

MATERIALS:

Harry the Happy Caterpillar Grows: Helping Children Adjust to Change by Cindy Jett, available from Amazon

A squishy, soft ball

Music

One copy of the *"Sample Change Questions"* worksheet

centerforloss.com
Worksheets.pdf
Page 53

A piece of 12" x 18" construction paper for each child

Markers and crayons

Changes, Changes, Changes

The death of someone loved creates many changes for surviving family members. For young children, these changes may include changes in relationships, routines, responsibilities, activities, and interests. The process of adapting and reacting to new life situations may take months or years.

GOAL:

To help the children understand that life will be different now that someone loved has died

ACTIVITY:

1. Ask the children what changes have taken place since the deaths.

2. Read aloud and discuss *Harry the Happy Caterpillar Grows.*

3. After reading, talk about the changes that occurred for Harry. Why didn't he want to change? What were his fears? What happened as a result of the changes?

4. Play the game On the Ball. Play music as the children toss a soft ball to each other. When the music stops, the child who has the ball should answer a change question. After the child answers the question, encourage other children to also respond. Continue with additional rounds.

5. After the game, hand out the construction paper to the children. Help them divide the paper into two columns. Label one column "Before" and the other "After."

6. In the Before column, have the children draw pictures of what life was like before the person died. If a child would like to have words with the drawings, help them if they need it.

7. In the After column, have the children draw pictures of what life is like after the person died. If a child would like to have words with the drawings, help them if they need it.

8. When the children finish, have them share their papers with the rest of the group.

Growth Flowers

(This activity may take two sessions. You may want volunteers to help.)

When a loved one dies, young children often feel that there will be so many missed opportunities for their loved one to witness their physical, emotional, academic, and social growth.

GOAL:
To show the children how much they have grown since the death and how they will continue to grow

ACTIVITY:
1. Talk about the different ways the children have grown since their loved one died. Encourage discussions about their physical, emotional, academic, and social growth.

2. Read and discuss *How Kids Grow*.

3. Hand out a small flowerpot to each child. They may paint this pot however they would like. When they are done, set the pots aside to dry.

4. Hand out four flower templates to each child. On each petal, with assistance from a volunteer, the children should write one way in which they have grown. Encourage the child to choose one flower each for physical, emotional, academic, and social growth.

5. They may now decorate their flowers and cut them out.

6. Glue each flower to a craft stick.

7. When the flowerpots are dry, fill them with floral foam to anchor the craft sticks.

8. Have each child share his or her flowerpot with the rest of the group.

9. If time remains at the end of either session, play the Consequences board game.

MATERIALS

How Kids Grow by Jean Marzollo, available from Scholastic.com

A small flowerpot for each child; try your local craft store

Paints for the pots; try your local craft store

Four flower templates for each child; FirstPalette.com has several options

Scissors

Markers and crayons

Craft sticks

Glue

Floral foam

Consequences board game, available from ChristianBook.com

MATERIALS:

I Want To Be Somebody New by Robert Lopshire, available from Amazon

Four different colors of construction paper; each child will need one piece of each color

Scissors

Crayons

Your Own Two Feet

Developmentally, young children are just beginning to develop their own identities. Now that someone they love has died, it is important that they continue to search for their identity despite the death. Thinking about the present and a bit about the future will help them on their path to discover who they are and how they fit into this world.

GOAL:
To help the children continue to develop their own self-identity even though someone they love has died

ACTIVITY:
1. Read aloud and discuss *I Want To Be Somebody New*.

2. After reading, ask the children if they ever want to be someone new and why.

3. Have the children trace their feet on four different colored papers (for example, pink, yellow, blue, and green).

4. Cut out each set of feet.

5. On the pink feet, have them draw one thing they love to do.

6. On the yellow feet, have them draw one thing that they miss about the person who died.

7. On the blue feet, have them draw one thing that has really changed since the people they love died.

8. On the green feet, have them draw one thing that they hope to do in the future (remember, the future may be as soon as tomorrow).

9. When everyone is done, have each child share his or her feet.

10. If time permits, set up a walking course with all of the feet. Let the children "walk the feet" as they read the comments on each foot.

Coat of Arms

When a loved one has died, children often question their self-identity. This may be due to the many changes occurring in the family and in the current life of the child. Talking about and analyzing these changes are important in order for the child to move on.

GOAL:

To help the children embrace the changing nature of their identities

ACTIVITY:

1. Talk with the children about how they are feeling about themselves lately. Do they feel they have changed since their loved one died? How are they feeling about this?

2. Read aloud and discuss *Spoon.*

3. After reading the book, discuss how they feel the same or different. Remind them how "different" does not mean something bad. Have they been singled out because of the death?

4. Hand out the "Coat of Arms" worksheet.

5. Let the children work on their personal coat of arms. They can write words, draw pictures, or choose other ways to illustrate on the paper what their coat of arms would look like.

6. When the children have finished, have them share their coats of arms with each other.

AGE GROUP:

Elementary

MATERIALS:

Spoon by Amy Krouse Rosenthal, available from Amazon

Copies of the "*Coat of Arms*" worksheet (print this on sturdy paper)

centerforloss.com
Worksheets.pdf
Page 54

Markers, crayons, and colored pencils

Other decorations, like stickers

Elementary

CLAY MOSAICS

MATERIALS:

Beginner's Guide to Mosaic by Alison Slater, optional, available from Amazon, or find examples of mosaics online

5" x 5" piece of sturdy cardboard for each child

Sculpey III Polymer Clay

Large heart-shaped cookie cutter, available at Michael's or your local craft store

110+ Assorted Colors C3 Recycled Glass Tiles (loose) from MosaicArtSupply.com

Mosaic Tiles

(There are two ways to do this activity.)

When someone loved dies, the self-concept of a child may change. This death often requires a child to take on new roles. Sometimes a renewed self-confidence in a child helps them to be more caring, understanding, and sensitive. To create a healthy reconstruction of the self, a child must:

• Be able to grieve openly in a way that is developmentally appropriate,

• Have open communication about the death and any other issues that arise,

• Reorganize/reexamine his or her self-concept after the death, and

• Become reinvested in his or her "new" life.

GOAL:

To have the children create a mosaic to represent their changed lives

ACTIVITY:

1. Talk with the children about how their lives have changed. Bring up places such as home, school, with friends, outside activities, with other relatives and adults.

2. Ask the children what the word mosaic means. A mosaic is a picture or decorative design made by setting small colored pieces, like stone, tile, or paper, onto a surface.

3. Show the kids the *Beginner's Guide to Mosaic* or the online examples of mosaics you found.

IF YOU WANT TO CREATE CLAY MOSAICS:

4. Give each child a 5" x 5" piece of sturdy cardboard.

5. Let the children choose the color of clay for their mosaic bases. Have them flatten the clay as much as possible onto the cardboard pieces.

6. Using a heart-shaped cookie cutter, help the children cut out their heart-shaped clay piece. Remove the excess clay.

7. Using loose mosaic tiles, let the children form designs or create a picture with their tiles representing who they feel they are after the death.

8. When they are done placing tiles, have the children share their mosaics with the rest of the group.

9. Bake the mosaics according to the directions on the package to hold the tiles in place. Return the mosaics to the children at the next session.

IF YOU WANT TO CREATE PAPER MOSAICS

(GlitteringShards.com is a good resource):

1. Give each child a piece of colored construction paper. Help them glue the paper to a piece of cardboard for stability.

2. Let the children form designs or create a picture with the ripped pieces of paper representing who they feel they are after the death.

3. When they have their design formed, help them glue each piece to the paper.

4. Have the children share their mosaics with the rest of the group.

PAPER MOSAICS MATERIALS:

Beginner's Guide to Mosaic by Alison Slater, optional, available from Amazon, or find examples of mosaics online

A piece of colored construction paper for each child

Cardboard to back the paper

Small ripped up pieces of scrapbook paper, old cards, and other paper

Glue

MATERIALS:

The Mixed-Up Chameleon by Eric Carle, available from Amazon

Copies of the "*Who Am I?*" worksheet

📄 centerforloss.com
Worksheets.pdf
Page 55

Magazines, optional

Scissors, optional

The Self Esteem Game, available from SelfHelpWarehouse. com

Who Am I?

When someone loved dies, the social and functional roles in the child's family may change. Also, the relationship to their loved one may have been a critical part of the child's self-identity. Thus, the child may be wondering "who am I now?"

GOAL:

To help the children explore who they are after the death of someone loved

ACTIVITY:

1. Talk about the changes that have occurred in their lives since the deaths.

2. Read aloud *The Mixed-Up Chameleon.*

3. Discuss the book in relation to the feeling of wanting to be someone or something different as a result of the death. Remind the children that this is very normal!!

4. Pass out copies of the "Who Am I?" worksheet.

5. In the first row, have the children put words into the columns. For example, under "Who was I?" a child might write the word "daughter." If her other parent is still alive, she may write "daughter" in the "Who am I now?" column. But if a child writes the word "happy" in the "Who was I?" column, he may write something like "sad" in the "Who am I now?" column. Let the children know that it's OK to write whatever they are feeling.

6. In the second row, the children may illustrate some of their thoughts or cut out pictures from magazines if you have them available.

7. If time remains, play The Self Esteem Game.

You're On the Ball

When a loved one dies, the actual physical death of a person is the primary loss experienced by the child. However, death is more than loss of the individual's physical presence. Changes may impact the child in significant ways, which include loss and change of self. Individuals are defined in many different ways. One's identity, self-confidence, sense and understanding of physical health, personality, and role in the family can be changed by a death.

GOAL:
To help the children embrace the changes happening to them in the present

ACTIVITY:
1. Discuss with the children how changes have affected them since the death of their loved ones.

2. Read aloud and discuss *Milton's Secret*.

3. Discuss the book, focusing on what it means to live in the present instead of the past or the future.

4. Play the game On the Ball. Play music as the children toss a soft ball to each other. When the music stops, the child who has the ball should answer a change question. After the child answers the question, encourage other children to also respond. Continue with additional rounds.

5. If time remains, play the game Stare.

AGE GROUP:
Elementary

MATERIALS:
Milton's Secret: An Adventure of Discovery through Then, When, and the Power of Now by Eckhart Tolle, available from Amazon

Squishy or foam ball

Music

"Sample Questions About Change" worksheet (feel free to add more)

 centerforloss.com Worksheets.pdf Page 56

Stare board game, available from Amazon

MATERIALS:

Copies of the *"Notes About Me"* worksheet

centerforloss.com
Worksheets.pdf
Pages 57 - 58

Copies of the *"How to Write a Personal Ad"* worksheet

centerforloss.com
Worksheets.pdf
Page 59

Pictures of the teens

Large pieces of paper

Glue

Colored pencils, markers, stickers, and other decorative objects

A Personal Ad

(At the session before this one, ask the teens to bring in pictures of themselves.)

When someone with whom a teen has had a relationship dies, the teen's self-identity naturally changes. A death often requires the teen to take on new roles that had been filled by the person who died.

GOAL:
To help the teens focus on the positive aspects of who they are as well as the many facets of their personalities

ACTIVITY:

1. Discuss with the teens the changes that have happened since the death. These changes may have occurred at home, within themselves, and in their friends group.

2. Explain what a personal ad is: an advertisement placed by an individual in a newspaper or other publication seeking something. Kind of like Missed Connections on Craigslist, but not as weird.

3. Hand out the "Notes About Me" worksheets and have the teens fill them in.

4. Explain to the teens that they will be advertising themselves to others. They should use the guidelines in the "How to Write a Personal Ad" worksheet and read through the personal ad sample.

5. Have the teens write their personal ad based on their "Notes About Me" worksheets.

6. When they are done, the teens can attach their personal ad and picture to a large piece of paper. If they want, they can decorate the paper.

7. Encourage the teens to share part of their personal ads with the rest of the group.

Crossing the Bridge

(This activity will probably take two sessions.)

As grieving teens question their own self-identities, they bring to light the question, "Where am I going and how will I know when I get there?" This often requires a "vision" and a plan for where they would like to go with their lives.

GOAL:
To help the teens find purpose and vision in their lives

ACTIVITY:

1. Before the session, you will need to create copies of the "Exploration to Prepare to Write the Personal Vision Statement," on pages 66-69.

2. Explain to the teens that a personal vision statement can help provide guidance for your life. It can provide the direction for your course of your life and help you make choices. Your personal vision statement is a light in the darkness when you have lost your way.

3. Pass out a copy of the "Personal Vision Statement" worksheet you created to each teen.

4. Reminding the teens that their personal vision statement may change over time, look at the written example of a personal vision statement on page 69.

5. Allow time for them to write their vision statement. (This may be the end of session one.)

6. Discuss the concept of "crossing the bridge." We cross a bridge during moments like the first day of school, moving into a new home, going back to school after the death, and making a difficult decision.

7. Hand out and discuss the poem "Crossing the Bridge" and the explanation.

8. Explain that they will be constructing a bridge as a metaphor for life and the many times we "cross over" from one state of being to another.

9. Pass out copies of the directions on how to make the bridge. Let the teens each create their own bridge. They can take them home or eat them.

MATERIALS:

Copies of the *"Exploration to Prepare to Write the Personal Vision Statement"* worksheet on pages 66-69

Copies of the poem *"Crossing the Bridge"* and accompanying explanation

 centerforloss.com
Worksheets.pdf
Page 60

Copies of the *"Directions for Building the Bridge"*

 centerforloss.com
Worksheets.pdf
Page 61

FOR EACH BRIDGE:

At least eight marshmallows, small or large

At least 12 raw spaghetti pieces

At least one raw linguine piece

Exploration to Prepare to Write the Personal Vision Statement

WORKSHEET

reprinted with permission from Susan M. Heathfield

Use these questions to guide your thoughts.

- What are the eight to ten things you most enjoy doing? Be honest. These are the eight to ten things without which your weeks, months, and years would feel incomplete.

  1. ....
  2. ....
  3. ....
  4. ....
  5. ....
  6. ....
  7. ....
  8. ....
  9. ....
  10. ....

- What three things must you do every single day to feel fulfilled in your life?

  1. ....
  2. ....
  3. ....

What are your five most important values or priorities?

1. ....

2. ....

3. ....

4. ....

5. ....

- Your life has a number of important facets or dimensions, all of which deserve some attention in your personal vision statement. Write one priority for each of these dimensions.

Physical ....

Spiritual ....

School ....

Family ....

Friends ....

Fun ....

- If you never had to go to school again in your life, how would you spend your time instead of going to school?

- When your life is ending, what will you regret not doing, seeing, or achieving?

- What strengths have other people commented on about you and your accomplishments? What strengths do you see in yourself?

- What weaknesses have other people commented on about you and what do you believe are your weaknesses?

Sample of a Personal Vision Statement

By Patricia Morrissey

My own personal vision statement includes such items as reading and writing every day; publishing books; sharing a lifetime of knowledge about people, management, and workplaces with a vast international audience; having a positive impact on every person with whom I come in contact; living daily a life dedicated to integrity, commitment, challenge, and joy; loving my husband and valuing my marriage; valuing a few close friends; valuing family relationships; being at all times aware of and engaged in my natural environment; inventing and writing about recipes and food; traveling the world to experience its richness; watching plays and movies; listening to music; never having to worry about spending money on anything I want; and walking by Lake Michigan.

When I live and experience the components of my personal vision statement frequently, I feel an inner peace and joy that knows no bounds. Your personal vision statement will have the same impact for you. Take the time to formulate answers to the above questions, and write your personal vision statement. Then, listen to your heart sing with the fullness of your articulated dreams.

Teens

Examples of personal mission statements, available from www.franklincovey.com/msb/inspired/wall or perform an internet search

Paper

Pens and pencils

Zobmondo!! Would You Rather...? board game, available from Amazon

Personal Mission Statement

When teens experience the death of someone loved, they often feel lost and question their own self-identities. Writing a personal mission statement often forces teens to think deeply about their lives, clarify their purpose, and identify what truly is important to them. A personal mission statement may also become part of the teens rather than something they only think about occasionally.

GOAL:
To help the teens develop their new self-identities by creating personal mission statements

ACTIVITY:
1. Ask the teens if they know what a personal mission statement is. During the development of a personal mission statement, you examine and evaluate the things you want, the person you are, the things you want to do, and the person you want to become.

2. Let the teens know that they will be thinking about and writing their own personal mission statements today.

3. Share examples of personal mission statements with the teens. Ask them what they think makes a good personal mission statement. A personal mission statement should be inspiring, encouraging them to become who they want to be and do what they want to do.

4. Have the teens think about what they want from life, what their talents are, what they value, and what they want to have accomplished by the end of their lives.

5. Let them write down their ideas and begin drafting a statement from those ideas. Encourage them to share some of their ideas with the rest of the group.

6. Before the next session, the teens should work on revising their personal mission statements into a more cohesive whole. You can begin the next session with a short discussion on how creating a personal mission statement has affected or will affect the way they think about the things they do.

7. If time remains, play Zobmondo!! Would You Rather...?

Teens

MATERIALS:

Copies of "Priorities" poem by Rebecca K. Drnjevic for each teen, available from authorsden.com

Copies of the "*List of Possible Priorities*" worksheet

centerforloss.com
Worksheets.pdf
Page 62

Five rocks for each teen

Metallic markers

Stickers

One plastic container for each teen; try Tupperware

Sand

One battery-operated tea light for each teen

Priorities, Rocks, and Sand

After the death of someone loved, teens will often question their self-identities. They may temporarily feel a heightened dependence on others, as well as feelings of helplessness, frustration, inadequacy, and fear. Awakening their priorities in life will hopefully assist them in developing a renewed sense of self.

GOAL:
To help the teens develop their new self-identities through identifying their priorities

ACTIVITY:

1. Hand out and read aloud the poem "Priorities."

2. Discuss priorities in general. Life priorities drive our lives and help define us.

3. Hand out the list of possible priorities to each teen and read through it.

4. Have each teen choose five priorities. They can be from the list or priorities the teen has come up with.

5. The teens can write these on the rocks using metallic markers. They may add drawings and stickers to these.

6. Place the rocks into a plastic container. The container may be decorated, but not too much, as the priority rocks should always be able to be seen.

7. Add some sand to the container. The sand stands for all those other things in their lives that may interfere with their priorities.

8. Place a battery-operated tea light on top of the rocks to signify that the teens' priorities should always be "lit up."

Search for purpose and meaning

When someone loved dies, the meaning and purpose of life will be questioned. Children and teens often ask the "How?" and "Why?" questions, such as "How could God let this happen?" "Why did God take my Mommy?" or "Why is my friend dead?"

The people who died were an important part of them. Sadness and loneliness are often the responses to the death of someone loved. Children and teens may feel that when this person died, part of them died also. Life may feel very empty.

Questioning the "why" and "how" of the death often leaves children and teens questioning their faith and beliefs. Many doubts may arise, which bring forth many questions.

The activities in this section are designed to assist children and teens in their search for meaning by looking at what happens in nature and examining how they are connected to nature and each other, considering their connection with a higher power, and thinking about their own life's purpose and meaning and spiritual growth.

The Temenis butterfly is your companion through the fifth need of mourning. Though butterflies instinctively know their part in life, grieving children and teens must be helped in their search for meaning after someone loved dies.

Remember to always think of the activity as the secondary task to accomplish for the group. The first task is to get the group members to express their grief and connect with each other. The game or activity is just a medium through which these tasks may be accomplished.

MATERIALS:

The Grandpa Tree
by Mike Donahue,
available from Amazon

Large sheet of paper

Markers and crayons

The Grandpa Tree

Understanding the "hows" and "whys" of death depends upon the developmental maturity and experience of the child. Often, the understanding of death is related to the way significant adults in their lives relate to the children. Using "teachable moments" when a child finds a dead animal or bird or becomes aware of the death of a loved one or the "nurturing moment" when death happens to a classmate, friend, or relative assists young children with the "hows" and "whys" of death. Sometimes the child does not verbalize this search for meaning but demonstrates it in art, play, or acting-out behaviors. The child may appear to be truly suffering as he/she goes through this search for meaning. A patient, non-judgmental adult can support the child as he/she learns to accept that there are things we cannot know and cannot have control over.

GOAL:
To help the children ask why questions and search for answers

ACTIVITY:

1. Ask the children if they know "why" death happens. What questions do they have about why someone they love died?

2. Read *The Grandpa Tree.*

3. Ask the following questions after reading the book:

   • How did the new little tree feel when it was growing up?

   • How did the tree feel when it was the biggest one in the forest?

   • Why did the Grandpa Tree fall down?

   • What did the Grandpa Tree do when it was on the ground?

   • Why did the Grandpa Tree feel so good about being on the ground?

   • How is the Grandpa Tree like a person who has died?

4. Using a large piece of paper, with the title "The Grandpa Tree," work together to create a group mural of the story. Decide ahead of time what will be on the mural and who is going to draw which part. When the mural is completed, have the kids decide on one sentence about the story and write it on the paper.

MATERIALS:

Happy To Be Me!: A Book About Self Esteem by Christine Adams, available from Amazon

One framed picture; content doesn't matter

One 8.5" x 11" white frame for each child, or you can make frames out of white foam board

One 9" x 12" piece of construction paper for each child

Markers and crayons

Tape

I am the Picture; My Loved One is the Frame

When a loved one dies, young children often ask many "Why" and "How" questions. Common questions are, "Why did God let my loved one die?" or "Where did my loved one go?" Answers to these questions often involve religion or spirituality, but always involve truth.

GOAL:

To help the children in their search for meaning by highlighting the qualities of the people who died that are present in them

ACTIVITY:

1. Talk about the physical attributes of each child. For example, color of hair and eyes, shape of nose, mouth, etc.

2. Read aloud and discuss *Happy To Be Me!*

3. Discuss the difference between what's on the outside and the qualities of each of us that are on the inside of the body.

4. Show a framed picture of something (or someone). Ask the children what they look at when they see a framed picture, the picture in the frame or the frame itself.

5. Hand out an 8.5" x 11" white frame to each child.

6. Also hand out a 9" x 12" sheet of construction paper to each child.

7. On the construction paper, have the children draw pictures of themselves doing different things, like being with a friend, reading a book, playing a game, snuggling with their parent(s), etc. Also help them write words around the drawing representing their qualities (both good and bad), such as I like to play, I am friendly, I am loving, I love music, I sometimes get mad, I don't like to eat asparagus, etc.

8. Decorate the outside of the frame with pictures

and words that remind them of the person who died.

9. Tape the drawing over the frame, explaining to the children that they are alive here on earth, and that the frame represents the person who died. Those people will always be with the children in some way, even if they aren't physically present.

10. What are some of the qualities that the children have in common with the people who died? What are qualities that they have but the person who died didn't?

11. Can the children see how the spirit of the person who died is living on in them?

MATERIALS:

The Brightest Star! by Kathleen Maresh Hemery, available from the Centering Corporation

CD player, iPod speakers, laptop, or DVD player

"Circle of Life" lyrics

📄 centerforloss.com
Worksheets.pdf
Page 63

Loaf of bread

Copies of the *"How I Am the Same"* worksheet

📄 centerforloss.com
Worksheets.pdf
Page 64

Lion King coloring sheets, available from coloring-book.info, search for "Lion King"

Markers and crayons

My Loved One Lives On in Me

GOAL:

To help the children in their searches for meaning after someone loved dies

ACTIVITY:

1. Read aloud and discuss *The Brightest Star!* by Kathleen Maresh Hemery.

2. Ask questions after the book, such as, "I wonder where the spirit of the person goes when someone dies?" or "I wonder what we can learn from nature about death?"

3. Play the song "Circle of Life" from the Lion King. If you have the soundtrack, play it from your CD or iPod. The song is also available on YouTube, and, if you want, you could show the Circle of Life scene on the Lion King DVD. Cater your choice to the kind of group you have.

4. Briefly discuss how all living things, including plants, animals, and humans, are born, live, and die. You can use lines from the "Circle of Life" to illustrate your points.

5. Take a whole loaf of bread and pull chunks from it. Be sure to vary the size and look of each chunk.

6. Give each child a piece of bread. Ask them if their pieces look the same. Help them see that each piece of bread contains identical ingredients. One piece does not have more salt or flour.

7. Explain that the pieces of bread are just like us. We are made up of the same basic stuff even though our shapes and sizes are different. The loaf of bread represents the children and the salt (or yeast or flour) in the bread represents the people who died. They are present in all pieces of the bread and present in each of the children.

8. Using the "How I Am the Same" worksheet, help the children fill it in with qualities that they have and that the people who died had. It is OK to list qualities they do not have in common.

9. If time remains, the children may color Lion King coloring sheets.

Finding Grandpa Everywhere

AGE GROUP:

Early Childhood

GOAL:

To give the children a place to ask questions and continue their search for meaning

ACTIVITY:

1. Ask the children what questions they have about death. Write these down on a large sheet paper.

2. Read aloud and discuss *Finding Grandpa Everywhere.*

3. Let the children know that in this session they are going to make a question box about death so that whenever they have questions, they can put them in this box and share it with an adult.

4. On the cover of the box, write the words My Question Box. (You can also write the child's name, for example Susan's Question Box.)

5. Allow the children to decorate their boxes using the supplied decorating materials.

6. As they conclude their decorating, ask each child what questions he or she would like to put into the box. Give each child a small pad of paper and pencil to include in the box so that there will always be materials nearby to write a question.

MATERIALS:

Finding Grandpa Everywhere: A Young Child Discovers Memories of a Grandparent by John Hodge, available from Amazon

Small cardboard boxes; try your local craft store

Markers

Stickers, scrapbooking supplies, and other decorations

Glue

A small pad of paper and a pencil for each child

MATERIALS:

Large sheet of paper

Three non-bendable straws for each child

About 20 small paper-clips for each child

Stars (or hearts, circles, etc.) cut out of heavy paper

Play-Doh or other clay-like substance

Connect Four, available from Amazon

Our Connection with the People Who Died

This "search for meaning" involves spirituality, which helps to explain the "Whys" and "Hows" of death for children. It also helps children know that they are connected to something greater than themselves, to the universe, nature, and the energy that flows through all of us. They are connected to every other child and adult on the planet, as well to the person who died.

GOAL:

To help the children visualize their connections to the people who died

ACTIVITY:

1. Ahead of time, cut out different shapes from heavy paper. Make them large enough so the children can hang them from a mobile.

2. Using a large sheet of paper, ask the children how they think we all are connected to each other. Write their responses on the paper.

3. Ask the children how they think we are connected to the people who died.

   Children will respond in many ways to the questions above. Some of them will very likely bring up a higher power. They may refer to the fact that we all have our differences, but on a spiritual level, our souls are all the same and come from the same source. Allow a healthy discussion to take place.

4. After the discussion, explain that they are going to make mobiles out of straws and paperclips to represent the ways we are connected to the people who died.

5. The straws and paperclips will represent the ways in which we are connected; the stars or other symbols will be the words we use to signify the connections.

6. Beginning with the paper symbols, have the children write one connection on each symbol. Set these aside.

7. To make the mobile:

- Slip a paperclip on the middle of a straw and one on either end of the straw. There should be three paperclips on the straw. Stick a small piece of Play-Doh on the end of the straw to keep the paperclips from falling off.

- Make a few of these units and put them together using paperclip chains of various lengths. To make the mobile balance, slide the paperclips around on the straw.

- Clip the paper symbols to the mobile.

- Add more paperclips to the top straw for a hanger.

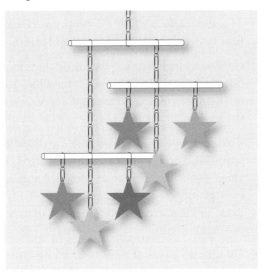

8. If time remains, play the game Connect Four.

MATERIALS:

Large sheet of paper

The Raindrop by Brian D. McClure, available from Amazon

Two clear plastic cups for each child

Two sets of small pieces of paper, using two different colors

Markers

Invisible Ink Pen & UV Light, available from Amazon

The Visible and Invisible Worlds

As children search for meaning regarding their loved one's death, the concepts of faith and hope often are introduced to children. These concepts are invisible. But often, faith is what draws children from the invisible to the visible. It helps children know that they are connected to something greater than themselves and to every other person on the planet.

GOAL:

To allow the children to explore their faith in "invisible" things as they search for meaning

ACTIVITY:

1. Using a large sheet of paper, ask the children what some of their "invisible" traits are. Invisible traits are things that people can't see on the outside. For example, they might say things like smart, loving, caring, funny, etc.

2. Read aloud and discuss the *The Raindrop*.

3. Talk about how the little raindrop really learned to have faith that he was important and valuable.

4. Give each child two clear plastic drinking cups, one marked "Visible," the other "Invisible." You can do this ahead of time so the cups are prepared for the session.

5. Using small pieces of paper, have the children write down on each piece things that are visible about them, like brown hair, friends, my green eyes, pictures of my Mom, clothes I wear, my tears, two feet, etc. Place these pieces of paper in the "Visible" cup.

6. Using small pieces of a different color paper, have the children write down things in their life that are invisible, especially related to the death, like how I feel inside, the spirit of my Dad, my hopes and dreams, my beliefs, my fears. Place these in the "Invisible" cup.

7. After defining the word faith as believing in something strongly, such as believing in a person or a higher power, analyze their "visible" items. Ask if they have faith that these things really exist. How do they know?

8. Looking at the items in the "invisible" cup, ask them if they have faith that these things are real. How do they know? Why are the invisible things so much more difficult to have faith in than the visible things?

9. Try and discuss what further invisible things in life they are having more difficulties with. Also, as a facilitator, make notes about these things so that another session might be devoted to more of the invisible.

10. If time remains, let the kids play with invisible ink pens and UV lights.

Elementary

MATERIALS:

Large sheet of paper

Becoming Me: A Story of Creation by Martin Boroson, available from Barnes & Noble

One piece of 12" x 18" construction paper for each child

Many different colored or decorative paper sheets of paper, cut into 1" x 18" strips

Scissors

Glue or tape

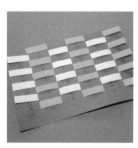

Weaving Our Beliefs

This "search for meaning" involves spirituality, which helps to explain the "Whys" and "Hows" of death for children. Children often have a better understanding of a higher power that watches over them than adults. It is this connection to "something greater" or a "higher power" that contributes to a child's sense of happiness. Often "happiness is the meaning and purpose in life, the whole aim and end of human existence," as Aristotle stated.

GOAL:

To help the children embrace their beliefs after someone loved dies

ACTIVITY:

1. Ahead of time, cut six width-wise slits in the 12" x 18" pieces of construction paper. Leave about one inch uncut on each side of the paper.

2. Ask the children what some of their beliefs are, especially related to the death. Write these down on a large sheet of paper. For example, the children might say "I believe that my Father is in heaven" or "I know that the spirit of my Mother is in my heart" or "When I hear the wind blow, I know my Grandmother is with me" or "When I hear my Grandpa's favorite music, I believe he is near me" or "I believe there is a God."

3. Read aloud and discuss *Becoming Me: A Story of Creation*.

4. Pass out the 12" x 18" pieces of construction paper to each child. Have each child choose six beliefs and write one on each of the six slits in his or her piece of construction paper.

5. Weave the strips of decorative paper in and out through the slits. Glue or tape each of these papers to the edge.

6. Make sure that every other row begins out and every other row begins inside. Move the strips of paper up as more are weaved into the mat.

7. Let the children know that the paper being weaved in and out represent those people, including the person who has died, in their lives who love and support them.

What Does Death Look Like?
What Does Life Look Like?

GOAL:

To help the children explore their beliefs about life and death

ACTIVITY:

1. Hand out copies of the Life and Death tables to the children.

2. Discuss some of the images they have of death and some beliefs or questions they also have about death. Have the children fill in the blanks on their tables with their images and beliefs. For example:

MATERIALS:

Copies of the "Life and Death" tables worksheet

 centerforloss.com
Worksheets.pdf
Page 65

Pens and pencils

Several colors of hard-drying clay

Permanent markers

Two CDs for each child

Images	Beliefs and Questions
Coffin	There is an afterlife.
A rainbow	Where does the body go?
A tree	My loved one lives on in me.

3. Discuss some of the images the children have of life as well as some of their beliefs and questions about it. Have them fill in the blanks on their tables with their images and beliefs. For example:

Images	Beliefs and Questions
Sun	How long will I live?
Being with friends	What does my future hold?
Music	It is important to have fun.

4. Give each child two blank CDs.

5. Label one CD "Life" and one CD "Death."

6. Let the children create their symbols of life and death on each CD using hard-dying clay or permanent markers.

7. When they are done, have the children share their CDs with the rest of the group.

8. Ask questions like, how are death and life alike? How are they different? What purpose does life have? What purpose does death have?

MATERIALS:

Fifteen index cards for
each teen, three cards
each of five colors

Copies of the *"Living
With No Regrets"* game
board

centerforloss.com
Worksheets.pdf
Page 66

One die

One game piece for
each teen (try using
pieces from Monopoly,
Sorry, the Game of Life,
or other games)

Living With No Regrets

When a teen loses a loved one, questions regarding meaning and purpose of life often arise. Even their philosophy of life and their religious beliefs may be challenged. Questions such as, "What does it mean to live a full and meaningful life?" and "What really matters in life?" are often asked. Teens are trying hard to find some meaning in their lives so that they can try and help themselves.

GOAL:
To help the teens find ways to continue living their lives with purpose

ACTIVITY:

1. Ask the teens if any of them have heard of or read the book *The Five Secrets You Must Discover Before You Die* by Dr. John Izzo. If any have, ask them to tell the group what it's about. If you want, you can pass around a copy of the book for the teens to look at, but it isn't necessary.

2. Izzo interviewed many older people (60+) who were identified by friends and acquaintances as "the one person they knew who had found happiness and meaning." He asked them questions like, "What brings you the most happiness in life, the greatest joy moment to moment?" and "What is the best advice you ever got from someone else about life? Did you take the advice? How have you used it during your life?"

3. Based on his interviews, he saw that there were five secrets generally agreed upon: 1) Be true to yourself; 2) Leave no regrets; 3) Become Love; 4) Live the moment, and 5) Give more than you take.

4. Let the teens know that in this session that they will be concentrating on leaving no regrets. Ask them how they might do that.

5. Offer life priorities as a way to leave no regrets. If you focus on your priorities and let them shape your decisions, there shouldn't be anything you regret doing or not doing.

6. If the teens have not already completed the activity "Priorities, Sand, and Rocks" (from Section 4), they each need to come up with five priorities (see the activity in Section 4 for how to identify these).

7. Hand out index cards to each teen. Make sure each teen gets three cards of five different colors.

8. Using the five priorities, each teen needs to ask three questions about this priority. For example, if one of the priorities is "Life Itself," some questions could be "How do you honor life?" "What does 'life itself' mean to you?" and "Why do you consider your life to be important?"

9. On the front of the index card, the priority should be listed. On the back of each card, one question should be written.

10. Hand out a game board to each teen. Explain how to play.

LIVING WITH NO REGRETS GAME

1. On the game, write down each of your priorities in three different places.

2. The oldest person gets to roll the die first.

3. Move your game piece as many squares ahead as reported on your die.

4. When landing on a priority square, draw a card that goes with that priority and answer the question.

5. The first one who gets to the end of the game board wins.

MATERIALS:

Copies of "*Viktor Frankl's Quotes*"

centerforloss.com
Worksheets.pdf
Page 67

Wood Senet game, available from Amazon

Search for Meaning

In attempting to relate the death of someone loved to a context of meaning, teens often turn to spirituality and religion so that they can find happiness and meaning.

GOAL:
To help the teens begin to find meaning in their lives after the loss of someone loved

ACTIVITY:

1. Ask the teens what "purpose and meaning" means to them right now, especially taking into account the deaths.

2. Relate the story of Viktor Frankl. You can look him up on Wikipedia or do an internet search to find more information.

   In 1946, a man by the name of Viktor Frankl chronicled his experiences as a concentration camp inmate and described his method of finding a reason to live. This book is titled *Man's Search for Meaning.* He stated that "I had wanted simply to convey to the reader by way of concrete example that life holds a potential meaning under any circumstance, even the most miserable ones." During WWII, Frankl lost most of his family in the concentration camps.

3. Pass out copies of Viktor Fankl's quotes and have the teens read them and pick two that speak to them.

4. After they all have chosen their quotes, have them share them and talk about them.

5. If time permits, play Senet.

Self, Life, Death, and Spiritual Well-Being

AGE GROUP:

Teens

This "search for meaning" involves spirituality, which helps to explain the "Whys" and "Hows" for teens. After a loved one dies, teens often have an urge to know themselves and their place in our universe. They want to experience themselves as a whole being, an individual. It is also important for teens to know that they are connected to something greater than themselves, to the universe, nature, the energy that flows through all of us.

GOAL:
To help the teens define what self, life, death, and spirit mean to them now

ACTIVITY:

1. Ask the teens if they know what a mandala is. Mandala means "circle" in Sanskrit and has become a generic term for a pattern that represents the cosmos, metaphysically or symbolically. Mandalas are used to aid meditation, focus attention, and establish a sacred space.

2. Using *Everyone's Mandala Coloring Book* or the images from the internet, display the many mandalas to the teens.

3. Let each teen choose a mandala they like that has room on the outside of the circle to write.

4. On the outside of the mandala, have the teens write the words "Self," "Life," "Spirit," and "Death." The mandala is now essentially divided into quarters.

5. In each quarter, have the teens write two or more words that represent the word on the outside of the mandala. Two words to represent "Self," two words to represent "Life," two words to represent "Spirit," and two words to represent "Death."

6. Have them choose one or two colors for each quarter and color it in.

MATERIALS:

Everyone's Mandala Coloring Book by Monique Mandali, optional, available from Amazon

Printouts of mandalas from the internet; try coloring-book.info

Colored pencils

7. When completed, ask the following questions:

   - What are your definitions of self, life, spirit, and death?

   - How are self, life, spirit, and death related?

   - What does this say about the universe?

8. Hopefully these and other questions raised by the teens and you as the facilitator will generate a discussion of spirituality and how the teens are connected to something greater than themselves, even if they don't believe in a god.

9. If time remains, allow the teens to color other mandalas.

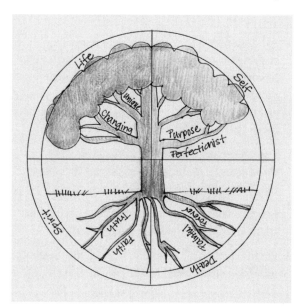

Fire in the Heart

In a quest to find purpose and meaning after the death of a loved one, teens often raise the "why" and "how" questions. This often leads is a higher need of having spiritual or religious answers. Therefore, the exploration of spirit, spiritual growth, and discovery are important to teens in their grief journey.

GOAL:
To give the teens a space to ask and answer some of the spiritual questions they may have regarding life and death

ACTIVITY:

1. If you have the resources, you may wish to purchase a copy for each teen to be read before this session. If not, one copy will suffice to introduce the teens to the concepts.

2. Introduce the book *Fire in the Heart: A Spiritual Guide for Teens*. You can find a synopsis on Amazon or Wikipedia or summarize from your reading of the book.

3. Pick out a portion of the book and read it aloud. If you have given this book to the teens, let them pick a favorite passage.

4. What does this book mean to the teens, especially as it relates to their lives now that someone loved has died? Hopefully a discussion will take place regarding the spiritual meaning of life.

5. Use the game Ker Plunk and the spirituality question cards. Before a teen can pull a stick out of the game, he or she must answer a question. Other members of the group can provide input. The point of this game is to have a discussion about the spiritual meaning of life, not to win.

AGE GROUP:

Teens

MATERIALS NEEDED:

Fire in the Heart: A Spiritual Guide for Teens by Deepak Chopra, available from Amazon

Ker Plunk

"Spirituality Questions" worksheet

centerforloss.com
Worksheets.pdf
Page 68

Receive continued adult support

In order to get through their grief journey, children and teens will always need the help of supportive adults in their lives. These adults can be helpful by caring, listening, and encouraging.

Many children and teens are abandoned shortly after the event of the death. "It's over and done with," "It's time to get on with your life," and "It's been two weeks now; aren't you over this?" are the types of messages directed at children and teens. These messages encourage children and teens to deny or repress their grief rather than express it.

To be truly helpful, the people in a support system for children and teens must appreciate the impact this death has had. They need to understand that in order to heal, children and teens must be allowed—even encouraged—to mourn long after the death.

The activities in this section are designed to help children and teens realize that there are people in their lives who truly want to care for and listen to them and that sometimes these people, especially adults, need to be someone other than their parent(s). Children and teens also need to recognize they may mourn differently than others, that the understanding of death is developmental, and that questions about the death may be asked over and over again.

The butterfly companion for the sixth need of mourning is the mourning cloak butterfly. The mourning cloak is a communal butterfly; caterpillars feed in groups and move in unison. Grieving children and teens also need the support of a community, even long after a death, if they are to reach reconciliation.

Remember to always think of the activity as the secondary task to accomplish for the group. The first task is to get the group members to express their grief and connect with each other. The game or activity is just a medium through which these tasks may be accomplished.

Early Childhood

MATERIALS:

A Little Bit of Trouble by Sally Grindley, available from Amazon

Tootsie Pop suckers (about five for each child)

Green ribbon

Hole punch

Scissors

Silk flowers, available from your local craft store or Lakeshore-Learning.com

A Little Bit of Trouble

Grief is a process, not an event. Grieving children will need adults in their lives long after the event of the death. Even those children who actively participate in the work of mourning will still mourn the loss in different ways as they pass through various developmental stages and on into adulthood. Adult caregivers can facilitate this mourning need by appreciating the impact of loss on children and allowing and encouraging a child to mourn long after the death.

GOAL:

To help the children appreciate the supportive adult presences in their lives

ACTIVITY:

1. Talk with the children about how they feel when they get into trouble. Ask them to share some stories, making sure they tell the entire ending, most specifically how the adults handled the situation and how the children felt about the outcome.

2. Read *A Little Bit of Trouble*.

3. Discuss how Grandfather Bear handled the trouble in the book. What did he say he was going to tell Mother? How did they think Mother was going to react?

4. Continue the discussion, specifically asking why the children think the adults in their lives react when they get into trouble. Why do the adults care when children are hurting physically and emotionally?

5. Because adults care so much for the well-being of a child, heartfelt "thanks you"s would certainly be appreciated by these adults.

6. Each child will make at least one Tootsie Pop heart flower craft to give to the adults in their lives who support them.

TOOTSIE POP VALENTINE FLOWER CRAFT FOR KIDS
Used with permission from thefrugalgirls.com

1. Pull the silk flowers apart, keeping the petals and discarding what you don't need. You can find silk flowers at second-hand stores, local craft stores, or Lakeshore Learning has them in packages of 500.

2. Decide which silk petals you would like to use. String them onto the end of the Tootsie Pop. You may have to make the hole in the middle of the flowers a little bigger to get them over the wrapper.

3. Tie about 12 inches of green ribbon below the silk flower petals to keep them from falling off. You can also tie a small card with a Valentine message on with the ribbon (if you are making the craft around Valentine's Day). Curl the ends of the ribbon with the scissors by pulling the ribbon over the edge of the scissors quickly.

Early Childhood

MATERIALS:

Kiss Good Night by Amy Hest, available from Amazon

A piece of drawing paper for each child

Markers and crayons

The Nurturing Game, available from SelfHelp-Warehouse.com

Creating a Safe Place To Be

It is very important for grieving children to feel safe, physically, emotionally, and socially. They need the presence of important adults in their lives as they pass through various developmental stages and on into adulthood.

GOAL:

To help the children identify safe places and people to go to as they grow

ACTIVITY:

1. Ask the children when it is that they feel scared. Have them describe some of these times, especially in relation to the death.

2. Read aloud and discuss *Kiss Good Night*.

3. Discuss the feeling of safety and what people and things make them feel safe.

4. Using pieces of drawing paper, have the children draw their favorite ways to feel happy and safe. Ask them to include their favorite toys and people in the picture.

5. Have each child share his or her drawing, allowing the child time to talk about it in detail.

6. If time permits, play The Nurturing Game.

Comforting Adults in My Life

GOAL:

To identify comforting adult presences in the children's lives

ACTIVITY:

1. Begin a discussion about what living things need to survive.

2. Read and discuss *Fireflies*, keeping in mind that fireflies, like all living things, need some basic things to survive, including air, water, and food.

3. After reading the book, ask the children if they were surprised that the fireflies were let go. Why or why not? What would have happened if the fireflies were kept in the jar?

4. Discuss again the basic needs of humans: other human beings, food, air, water, shelter, clothes. Can the kids think of any others?

5. Focus on the need for other human beings and ask the children who comforted them after the death and which adults continue to comfort them. Ask them questions such as, "How does it feel to be comforted?" and "How do the adults in your life comfort you?" and "Who are the main adults in your life who comfort you?

6. Using the "Comforting Adults" worksheets, help the children complete the sentences and draw illustrations for each section.

7. If time remains, play The Ungame using the kids' cards.

AGE GROUP:

Early Childhood

MATERIALS:

Fireflies by Julie Brinckloe, available from Amazon

Copies of the *"Comforting Adults in My Life"* worksheet

centerforloss.com
Worksheets.pdf
Page 69

The Ungame, available from Amazon

MATERIALS:

The Purple Balloon by
Chris Raschka, available
from ChristianBook.
com

Copies of the *"Support-
ive People in My Life"*
worksheet

centerforloss.com
Worksheets.pdf
Page 70

Several colors of large
pompoms

Glue

Feelings Bingo game,
available from Speech-
TherapyGames.com as a
free download

The Purple Balloon

GOAL:

To remind the children of all the helpful people they
have in their lives who can help them with their grief

ACTIVITY:

1. Read *The Purple Balloon.*

2. After reading the book, ask some "I wonder"
   questions, like:

   • I wonder if you have ever felt alone or sad?

   • I wonder if you have ever had a pet die?

   • I wonder if you know of anyone else who has
     died?

   • I wonder if you can name all the people who
     helped you when your loved one died?

3. Using the "Supportive People in My Life"
   worksheets, assist each child in filling in up to five
   names of those people who help him or her. These
   can be people who help with homework or chores
   but hopefully will be people the child finds helpful
   with his or her grief.

4. Have the children choose their balloon colors
   and glue a large pompom of that color onto each
   balloon.

5. If time remains, play Feelings Bingo.

NEED #6: RECEIVE CONTINUED ADULT SUPPORT

Appreciating Others

When children experience the death of someone loved, it is important for them to have adults in their lives to assist them with their grief journeys. Adult caregivers can facilitate this mourning need by appreciating the impact of loss on children and allowing and encouraging a child to mourn long after the death. In return, children who are fortunate to have supportive adults in their lives may want to show appreciation to these people for listening to them and helping to guide their journeys.

GOAL:

To help the children show appreciation for those adults who have helped them in their grief journeys

ACTIVITY:

1. Discuss the word "appreciate," especially in terms of what the children can do to show appreciation to the adults in their lives who assist them, especially with their grief journeys .

2. Read aloud and discuss *Have You Filled a Bucket Today?*

3. Using the "Appreciation of Others" worksheets, have the children complete their thoughts about the appreciation of those people in their lives who are helping them with their grief. They may include drawings after the words are completed.

4. If time remains, play The Ungame.

AGE GROUP:

Elementary

MATERIALS:

Have You Filled a Bucket Today?: A Guide to Daily Happiness for Kids by Carol McCloud, available from Amazon

Copies of the *"Appreciation of Others"* worksheet

 centerforloss.com
Worksheets.pdf
Pages 71 - 72

Pencils

Crayons and markers

The Ungame, available from Amazon

MATERIALS:

People Who Care About You: The Support Assets by Pamela Espeland and Elizabeth Verdick, available from Amazon

Ker Plunk, available from Amazon

"Questions for Ker Plunk" worksheet

centerforloss.com
Worksheets.pdf
Page 73

Explore Your Emotions coloring book, available for free download from alleghenycounty.us; search for "explore your emotions"

Markers and crayons

My Grief Support System

Grieving children will need adults in their lives even long after the event of the death. Even those children who actively participate in the work of mourning will still mourn the loss in different ways as they pass through various developmental stages and on into adulthood.

GOAL:

To let the children explore their support system following the death of someone loved

ACTIVITY:

1. Ask the children who the adults are in their life that they can talk to when they are feeling sad or angry about the death.

2. Read aloud and discuss *People Who Care About You*.

3. Using the game Ker Plunk, have each child answer a question before removing a stick. Other children in the group may also respond to the question.

4. If time permits, have the children work on pages from the Explore Your Emotions coloring book.

The Game of Support

When someone loved dies, life is changed forever. The balance that might have been there before the death is often thrown out of whack. Children feel great distress and really need supportive adults in their lives during this time. This is when the networks that have been created need to be strengthened. This could include parent/child relationships, grandparent/child relationships, and other adult/child relationships.

GOAL:

To help the children identify helpful and unhelpful ways people support them

ACTIVITY:

1. Ahead of time, print out the Game of Support questions and stick them on index cards or other heavy paper.

2. Talk with the children about which relationships in their lives are strong, meaning that they know they will be heard if they talk to those people. Why are these people better at listening than others? What do they do that is different from other adults?

3. Read aloud and discuss *The Great Kapok Tree.*

4. After reading the story, ask the children what the importance of the child from the Yanamomo tribe was. What would have happened if the man had not listened to the child?

5. Hand out one game board to each child.

6. They may glue this game board to a piece of construction paper. (You can also do this ahead of time.)

7. The youngest person begins the game.

8. Roll one die and advance that many spaces. When you land on a space, follow the directions and read a card. The question should first be answered by the player and then opened up to the other

AGE GROUP:

Elementary

MATERIALS:

The Great Kapok Tree: A Tale of the Amazon Rain Forest by Lynne Cherry, available from Amazon

Copies of *"The Game of Support"* game board

 centerforloss.com Worksheets.pdf Page 74

9" x 12" pieces of colored construction paper

Glue

"The Game of Support Questions," printed on index cards or heavy paper

centerforloss.com Worksheets.pdf Page 75

One die

One game piece for each child (try using pieces from Monopoly, Sorry, the Game of Life, or other games)

players. If a child cannot answer a question, then allow another child to answer for him or her. As a facilitator, add additional information or questions when appropriate.

9. The person who has exactly the correct die number to reach the end is the winner.

10. If time permits, play the game again.

Where are the Supports in My Life?

Grieving children will need adults in their lives long after the event of the death. They will also need an entire interpersonal support structure involving their family, friends, school, outside organizations, facilitators of a grief group, counselors, and themselves. The question of "Who will be there for me?" is a concern for most children.

GOAL:

To remind the children, now and in the future, of all the support they are receiving

ACTIVITY:

1. Ahead of time, create booklets for each child of "The Supports in My Life."

2. Using a large sheet of paper, divide the paper into three sections: people, actions, and words. Record answers to the questions "Who are the people in your life who support you?", "What types of actions from other people have supported you?" (i.e. hugs, people listening, etc.), and "What words have been most comforting to you as you mourn?"

3. Read aloud and discuss *Sam's Dad Died.*

4. Hand out "The Supports in My Life" booklets. Talk about each of the pages in the book and let the children complete the pages and color the pictures.

AGE GROUP:

Elementary

MATERIALS:

Large sheet of paper

Sam's Dad Died: A Child's Book of Hope Through Grief by Margaret M. Holmes, available from Amazon

Copies of *"The Supports in My Life"* booklet

centerforloss.com Worksheets.pdf Pages 76 - 78

Markers, crayons, and colored pencils

One small gift bag for each teen, available from BagsAndBows Online.com or your local craft store

Decorating supplies, like fabric paint, ribbon, gems, markers, etc.

Glue

Scissors

Copies of the *"Positive Self-Talk Messages"* worksheet

centerforloss.com
Worksheets.pdf
Page 79

Gift Bag

As teens cope with the death of someone loved, they will need adults in their lives even long after the event of the death. Adult caregivers can facilitate this mourning need by appreciating the impact of the loss on the teen and allowing and encouraging the teen to mourn long after the death. One of the ways in which they can help most is in promoting "self-talk" for the teens. This stresses the importance of assisting the teen with the internalization of positive messages.

GOAL:

To promote good self-talk with the teens

ACTIVITY:

1. Ahead of time, print out copies of the Positive Self-Talk Messages for teens. You may want to print it on colored or decorative paper.

2. Ask the teens what intangible gifts the person who died gave them. What intangible gifts have other adults given them?

3. Ask the teens if any of them talk to themselves, either out loud or inside their heads. When does this happen most and what type of talk is it?

4. Most people do carry on silent conversations with themselves. These conversations are called "self-talk." Generally, the same messages are repeated over and over until they are part of a person's beliefs. Negative self-talk makes people feel bad about themselves, but positive self-talk can help people feel better about themselves and what they can do.

5. Hand out a small gift bag to each teen. They may decorate this bag.

6. Hand out the "Positive Self-Talk Messages" to each teen. They can choose from those messages or write their own to put in their bag.

7. Encourage the teens to take the gift bag home and read through these messages in times of need.

8. You may also wish to encourage the teens to share the gift bag with supportive adults in their lives who can help them promote good self-talk.

Starbursts

When teens experience the death of someone loved, caring adults such as parents, teachers, counselors, or friends can help them during this time. If adults are open, honest, and loving, experiencing the loss of someone loved can be a chance for young people to learn about both the joy and pain that comes from caring deeply for others.

GOAL:
To let the teens open up about their support systems since the deaths

ACTIVITY:
1. Ahead of time, print and cut out the the Starburst Game cards. You can print them on colored paper or write the color on the back of the card.

2. Talk with the teens about their relationships with significant adults in their lives. Who are these adults? Which ones are most easy to talk with and why? Which ones are most difficult to talk with and why? What types of messages are they receiving from adults in their lives?

3. Ask the teens what they most want when having a conversation with an adult. You will probably hear things like:
   - simply listen and understand what I am going through without offering advice or commentary.
   - give permission or support for something.
   - offer advice or help.
   - guide me back on track if I'm in trouble, but in a way that's fair, consistent, and without harsh criticism or put-downs.

4. Distribute copies of the poem "On Listening." Read it aloud and have the teens react to this poem.

5. Play the Starburst Game by making four groups of colored cards that coordinate with the four flavors of the Starburst candies. Red cards = cherry; pink cards = strawberry; yellow cards = lemon; orange cards = orange. Each teen gets to eat a Starburst candy that coordinates with the color card that he or she answers.

AGE GROUP:

Teens

MATERIALS:

Copies of the poem *"On Listening"* by Ralph Roughton, M.D.; several versions can be found by doing an internet search

Starburst candies

"Starburst Game Cards" worksheet

centerforloss.com
Worksheets.pdf
Pages 80 - 87

Starburst game reprinted with permission by Gay McWhorter, author of Healing Activities for Children in Grief

MATERIALS:

Copies of the two
"Faces" worksheets

centerforloss.com
Worksheets.pdf
Page 88 - 91

The Faces game from
Buffalo Faces, available
from Amazon

The Way I Want to Be

When a teen experiences the death of a loved one,
they need to know that there are supportive adults in
their lives. The adults that teens best respond to tend
to be those who choose to be companions on the
grief journey rather than trying to direct it.

GOAL:
To help the teens identify adults in their lives who
can help them transform into who they want to be

ACTIVITY:
1. Discuss with the teens how their lives currently
   are going and what changes they would make to
   become more of who they want to be.

2. On one of the "Faces" worksheets provided, have
   the teens write down some of the aspects of their
   current lives.

3. On the other "Faces" worksheet, have the teens
   answer the question "How do I want my life to
   be?"

4. When they are done, discuss the two faces for
   each teen.

5. Ask the following questions and discuss:

   • How are you going to get from the way it is to
     the way you want it to be?

   • What do you need to do differently in order to
     get there?

   • Which adults in your life can assist you?

   • Which friends can assist you?

   • What barriers are in your way?

   • What is an action plan that you could develop
     to get to where you want to be?

   • How do you think you'll feel when you get to
     where you want to be?

6. If time remains, play the Faces game.

Timelines

Teen years are already tumultuous years, and the bereaved teen needs special attention. Under ordinary circumstances, teenagers go through many changes in their body image, behavior, attachments, and feelings. As they break away from their parents to develop their own identities, conflicts often arise within the family system. Life becomes even more complex when a father, mother, or other significant person dies.

GOAL:

To remind the teens that adult support was, is, and will be a large part of their lives

ACTIVITY:

1. Begin a discussion about the significant events in the lives of each of the teens since they were born. Begin the thinking with events such as being born, first teeth, walking, talking, first day of school, losing the first tooth, etc. Encourage the teens to think about other significant events in their lives such as other deaths, moving, first friend, first date, etc.

2. Using the "Important Events" worksheets, have the teens write down 12–15 important events in their present lives and six events that they hope will happen in their futures.

3. Let them transfer their events to the "Personal Timeline" worksheets.

4. When they have completed this task, ask them to look at it and count the number of times in both the present and future timeline where they needed or anticipate needing the support of an adult. For 15 present events and six future events (for an approximate total of 21 events), compute the percentage of time that this adult presence was and is needed. (Example: If adult support were needed for 10 of the 21 events, that would be 48 percent of important events.)

5. Discuss these results and what they signify with the teens. Remind them that it's OK to need the help of adults from time to time.

6. If time remains, play the game Would You Rather..?

AGE GROUP:

Teens

MATERIALS:

Copies of the *"Important Events"* worksheet

centerforloss.com
Worksheets.pdf
Page 92

Copies of the *"Personal Timeline"* worksheet

centerforloss.com
Worksheets.pdf
Pages 93 - 94

Pencils and pens

Zobmondo!! Would You Rather..? game, available from Amazon

Icebreakers

Reprinted with permission from Vanessa Van Petten of RadicalParenting.com

HUMAN WEB

Suggested age group: Early childhood, Elementary, Teens

For this game you separate the boys and girls into two groups (hopefully, they will end up being somewhat equal). Have each group hold hands, forming a circle, and then have them all walk forward until they are close together and the circle is small and tight. Drop hands. Now each kid should grab any two different hands except for those of his immediate neighbor. This will form a colossal mess! Next comes the fun part! The kids need to untangle themselves *without letting go of any hands*. They will have to step over arms, duck under, and work at it, but it is fun and challenging!

MUMMY GAME

Suggested age group: Elementary, Teens

For this game you need two rolls of toilet paper and six volunteers (three boys and three girls). Select one boy and one girl to become the "mummies;" the remaining volunteers will be the "embalmers." At your prompt, the embalmers will begin to quickly wrap the mummies with the entire roll of toilet paper. Encourage them to be careful not to tear the paper. The first team to finish the entire roll wins.

If you have a large group, you can split the kids into more than two groups, but you'll need more rolls of toilet paper.

EGG RACE

Suggested age group: Elementary, Teens

For this one you need two hard-boiled eggs and two spoons. You can either allow all of your children to participate in this relay, or you can just choose four to six kids for each team (depending on your time factor and the size of the group). As soon as you say "GO!", one runner from each team is to run to the designated point, carefully holding the egg on a spoon, and then return to the starting point and exchange the spoon with the next runner. The first team with all its participants back to the starting point wins.

If all the kids are participating, then you can divide them into two teams and let them walk/run the egg to their teammates across the room, eliminating the necessity of having to return the egg to where they started.

KNOBBY KNEES

Suggested age group: Elementary, Teens

For this icebreaker you will need two quarters and two jars (like quart canning jars). Ask for two volunteers, one boy and one girl, and have them attempt to drop the quarter into the jar positioned below them. The catch: they must hold the quarter between their knees.

KNOBBY KNEES II

Suggested age group: Early childhood, Elementary, Teens

This is a relay icebreaker, and you will need a blown-up balloon for each team. Simply have them clamp the balloon between their knees, run/waddle to the finish line, and race back to exchange the balloon with the next person on their team. First team to have all participants back to the starting line wins. Warning: Use discernment if you have girls wearing tight, straight skirts!

BABY FEED

Suggested age group: Early childhood, Elementary, Teens

Warning: messy icebreaker! You will need two of each of the following: bibs, blindfolds, jars of baby food, and baby spoons. Select teams of two boys and two girls. Have one person from each team sit in a chair with his or her partner standing behind the chair. The person sitting down must don the bib, and the standing partner will wear the blindfold. When you say "Go!", the blindfolded participants must feed the baby food to their partners from behind. The first team to drain the jar wins.

PICKLE PUCKER

Suggested age group: Elementary, Teens

For this icebreaker you will need two dill pickle spears and two packets of lemon Kool-Aid (go for the no sugar added kind; the generic brand is just fine). Choose the most sour looking boy and girl to participate. (Alternately, ask for volunteers who always wanted to be on Fear Factor!) It's very easy; all the participants have to do is dip their pickles into their Kool-Aid and devour! Oh, but is this super sour! They must dip after each bite. First one to finish the pickle wins.

DRAW FROM THE WELL

Suggested age group: Elementary, Teens

This is a relay icebreaker, so divide the kids into two teams (you can use all of your kids, or if you have too many, just select five or so for each team). Across the room you will have two clear, empty cups or glasses sitting on a table, one for each team. The teams will line up behind a bucket of water with the first person in each line holding a spoon. When you say "Go!" they will fill their spoons with water from the bucket and quickly transport it to the cups across the room. Then they will run back and hand off the spoon to the next in line. First team to fill their cup wins.

CLOTHESPINS

Suggested age group: Early childhood, Elementary, Teens

For this icebreaker you will need two clothes hangers with 20 clothespins randomly clamped all over each of them. Choose two students to play. When you say "Go!", they must remove as many clothespins as possible *with one hand* without dropping or putting any of them down. Whenever someone drops a clothespin, stop and count up the total for each. Whoever has the most is the winner.

BUBBLE BELCH

Suggested age group: Elementary, Teens

For this icebreaker you will need two cans of soda and two pieces of firm bubble gum. (The individually wrapped, pink kind works well.) Divide the group in half and let each team select a volunteer. The chosen two must swig an entire can of soda and then pop the gum into their mouths and chew it up. First one to blow a bubble wins!

It's funny because they will struggle with belching up the soda while they're trying to chew and blow!

FRISBEE LEAK

Suggested age group: Teens

For this icebreaker you will need two Frisbees and two glasses or bottles of water. Divide the group in half and select four or six participants from each. Send half of each team to one side of the room and half to the other. The object is to walk across the room with a Frisbee on your head and pass it off to the next team member, back and forth until everyone has gone. The catch: the Frisbee is full of water!

BALLOON OVER AND UNDER

Suggested age group: Early childhood, Elementary, Teens

For this icebreaker you will need two blown-up balloons. Divide the students into equal teams. Each team must stand in a single file line with about a foot between each of them. Hand an inflated balloon to the first person on each team. When you say "Go," they must pass the balloon backwards over their heads to the team members behind them. Those people then pass it through their legs to the next person in line. They must alternate over and under. The first team to get the balloon to the last person in line wins.

T.P. OVER AND UNDER

Suggested age group: Elementary, Teens

For this icebreaker you will need two rolls of toilet paper. Divide your group into two teams (or just select 10 children to play, if you want to keep it small and simple) and line them up, one in front of the other. Give the first person in each line a roll of toilet paper and instruct them to loosely unroll some and *carefully* pass it under their legs to the people behind them. Those people then pass it over their heads to the next in line. They must alternate under and over. The first team to get the unbroken toilet paper back to the front of the line wins.

MOUNT BUBBLE GUM

Suggested age group: Elementary, Teens

Warning: messy icebreaker! For this icebreaker you will need canned whipped cream (2-3 cans), paper plates, and individually wrapped bubble gum. You might also want to have on hand wet cloths or baby wipes to clean up the mess (or large bibs, if you're more into prevention). Select two or three kids to compete against one another. Each of them will be placed behind a table containing a nice, big mound of whipped cream with a piece of bubble gum hiding in the middle. They must locate their gum *with their faces only* (you might have to tie hands behind backs) and blow a bubble as quickly as possible. This is very challenging even once the gum is discovered because the wet, sugary cream makes the gum really soggy and goopy. Make sure that the cream is refrigerated and shaken well. Also, don't spray it until *immediately* before the game; otherwise your mountain will be a marsh!

WHISTLE CHALLENGE

Suggested age group: Early childhood, Elementary, Teens

For this icebreaker you will only need a package of saltine crackers. Select volunteers (three to five is adequate) who know how to whistle. Give them each two crackers and instruct them to chew them as quickly as possible and then try to whistle. The first to clearly whistle gets the prize. Beware: you may get showered with cracker crumbs!

SHOE SCRAMBLE

Suggested age group: Early childhood, Elementary, Teens

For this icebreaker you will need to divide the group into two teams (you can do boys v. girls, if the numbers are about even). They must all take off their shoes and put them in a pile. Mix the shoes up as they form an even circle around the pile. On your command, they must quickly dig out their shoes and put them back on their feet. First team to have all the correct shoes on their feet wins.

COTTON BALL SCOOP

Suggested age group: Early childhood, Elementary, Teens

For this icebreaker you will need two large bowls filled with cotton, two empty bowls, two blindfolds, and two spoons. Choose two participants, blindfold them, and give them 30 seconds to transfer as many cotton balls as possible into the empty bowl using only the spoon (no help from their other hand!). It's hilarious because they feel like they are lifting air and often are scooping and transferring nothing at all on the spoon! The other kids really enjoy watching this one.

BOBBING FOR DONUTS

Suggested age group: Elementary, Teens

For this icebreaker you will need a doughnut and a piece of string for each team. You may choose to select just a few kids to play, or if you're really brave (or "insane"), you might let all of them participate! You will seat half of the participants and have their partners stand behind them. The standing partner must string up a doughnut and hold it over the head of the seated partner. The seated one must then eat the doughnut off the string—no hands! The trick is to not let the doughnut fall!

HULA CHAIN

Suggested age group: Elementary, Teens

For this breaker you will need two Hula-hoops. This one involves all the kids (unless you want to hand pick ten or so for each team, if you have a really large group). Line the teams up down opposite walls, facing each other. But don't stand the children too close to the wall; they'll need room to maneuver. Have the team members hold hands, creating two long chains. Start the Hula-hoops at one end of each team. The object is to maneuver the Hula-hoop down the chain without letting go of hands. They just have to wiggle and squirm it over their arms, shoulders, and head!

NEEDLE IN A HAYSTACK

Suggested age group: Elementary, Teens

For this icebreaker you will need two bowls of rice with 20 paperclips dispersed throughout each one and two blindfolds. Blindfold a representative from each team. They will have 60 seconds to find as many paperclips as possible in the bowls of rice. Have their teams cheer them on and count down with you when the time gets down to only 10 seconds left. The person with the most paperclips found wins the game! Should the two tie, select another person from each group to play and rebury the paperclips. If it felt too easy, add more paperclips!

AIR, LAND, AND SEA

Suggested age group: Early childhood, Elementary, Teens

For this icebreaker you will simply need a masking tape line across the floor. Select three or four participants for each team and stand them behind the line. If you have a small enough group, allow all the children to participate! Explain that they are standing on "land," but when you say "sea," they are to jump across the line, and when you say "air," they are to jump straight into the air. When they are on the "sea" side, you say "land" to make them jump backward across the tape back onto land. If anyone touches the line or jumps the wrong way (i.e. crosses the land on "air"), they have to sit down. Give them a couple of practice runs before you begin the actual competition.

TEAM WORK

Suggested age group: Elementary, Teens

For this icebreaker you will need a small box containing two prizes, a sheet of gift-wrapping paper, and scotch tape for each pair of participants. Select six to eight kids and pair them off. The couples must cooperatively wrap a gift while they each have one hand behind their backs! The first pair to finish gets to keep the box and its contents.

PONY EXPRESS

Suggested age group: Early childhood, Elementary, Teens

For this icebreaker you will need two "stick" ponies—the kind that kids straddle between their legs and gallop around on. You don't need to get anything crazy; a stick with a bandana could work. Divide the children into two teams and pick one kid from each teem to "race" on the ponies. If you really want to make it crazy, give them a more complex racetrack to maneuver. Encourage their teams to cheer them on!

BUZZ BOMB BALLOON

Suggested age group: Elementary, Teens

For this icebreaker you will need a balloon for each participant (not blown up) and some type of target, which could be virtually anything (a chair, a book, etc.). You can either let all of the children participate, or just select a few from each side. Have the children stand in a circle around the target—about 10 feet away from it—or stand in a line with their team, facing the other team with the target in between. Each participant will blow up the balloon and pinch it shut without tying a knot. To keep from getting the balloons confused, you will either want to hand out different colors or write initials on them with a permanent marker. When you give the signal, all of the kids will let go of their balloons. The child whose balloon lands closest to the target wins.

LIFE SAVER

Suggested age group: Elementary, Teens

For this icebreaker you will need a Life Savers candy and a toothpick for each child. You can have as many teams as you want. Line each team up so that the children are side by side. Instruct them to hold the toothpick in their mouths—no hands allowed for this game! Put a Life Saver on the toothpick up the first person in each team line. They must pass the Life Saver from toothpick to toothpick down the line without using their hands. The first team to reach the end of the line with their Life Saver wins.

FRISBEE TOSS

Suggested age group: Early childhood, Elementary,

For this icebreaker you will need two Hula-hoops and six Frisbees. Suspend the Hula-hoops from the ceiling or have helpers hold them up in the air. Divide your group in half and select a few participants from each side. Let each player have three chances to toss a Frisbee into a Hula-hoop. You can assign different point values to each Hula-hoop or give more points for making a shot from farther away. The team that ends with the most points wins.

Materials

A Boy and a Bear: The Children's Relaxation Book by Lori Light, available from Amazon

A Little Bit of Trouble by Sally Grindley, available from Amazon

Becoming Me: A Story of Creation by Martin Boroson, available from Barnes & Noble

Beginner's Guide to Mosaic by Alison Slater, available from Amazon

Everyone's Mandala Coloring Book by Monique Mandali

Finding Grandpa Everywhere: A Young Child Discovers Memories of a Grandparent by John Hodge, available from Amazon

Fire in the Heart: A Spiritual Guide for Teens by Deepak Chopra, available from Amazon

Fireflies by Julie Brinckloe, available from Amazon

Gentle Willow by Joyce C. Mills, available from Amazon

Happy to Be Me!: A Kid's Book about Self-Esteem by Christine Adams, available from Amazon

Harry the Happy Caterpillar Grows: Helping Children Adjust to Change by Cindy Jett, available from Amazon

Have You Filled a Bucket Today?: A Guide to Daily Happiness for Kids by Carol McCloud, available from Amazon

How Kids Grow by Jean Marzollo, available from Scholastic.com

I Feel Orange Today by Patricia Godwin, available from Barnes & Noble

I Heard Your Daddy Died by Mark Scrivani, available from the Centering Corporation

I Miss You: A First Look at Death by Pat Thomas, available from Amazon

I Want to Be Somebody New by Robert Lopshire, available from Amazon

I'll Always Love You by Hans Wilhelm, available from Amazon

I'm Gonna Like Me: Letting Off a Little Self-Esteem by Jamie Lee Curtis, available from Amazon

Is a Worry Worrying You? by Ferida Wolff, available from Amazon

Kiss Good Night by Amy Hest, available from Amazon

Lifetimes by Brian Mellonie, available from Amazon

Milton's Secret: An Adventure of Discovery through Then, When, and the Power of Now by Eckhart Tolle, available from Amazon

My, Oh My—A Butterfly!: All About Butterflies by Tish Rabe, available from Amazon

People Who Care About You: The Support Assets by Pamela Espeland and Elizabeth Verdick, available from Amazon

Sam's Dad Died: A Child's Book of Hope Through Grief by Margaret M. Holmes, available from Amazon

Sarah Jane's Missing Smile by Julie Kaplow and Donna Pincus, available from Amazon

Something Small, a Sesame Street Book, printable from sesamestreet.org

Sometimes I Am Bombaloo by Rachel Vail, available from Amazon

Spoon by Amy Krouse Rosenthal, available from Amazon

Sweet, Sweet Memories by Jacqueline Woodson, available from Amazon

The Brightest Star! by Kathleen Maresh Hemery, available from the Centering Corporation

The Feelings Book by Todd Parr, available from Amazon

The Grandpa Tree by Mike Donahue, available from Amazon

The Great Kapok Tree: A Tale of the Amazon Rain Forest by Lynne Cherry, available from Amazon

The Memory Box by Kirsten McLaughlin, available from the Centering Corporation

The Mixed-Up Chameleon by Eric Carle, available from Amazon

The Patchwork Quilt by Valerie Flourney, available from Scholastic. com

The Purple Balloon by Chris Raschka, available from Christianbook. com

The Raindrop by Brian D. McClure, available from Amazon

Water Bugs and Dragonflies by Doris Stickney, available from Amazon

Water Bugs and Dragonflies coloring book, available from Barnesandnoble.com

What to Do When You Worry Too Much: A Kid's Guide to Overcoming Anxiety by Dawn Huebner, available from Amazon

When I Miss You by Cornelia Maude Spelman, available from Amazon

Where Do People Go When They Die? by Mindy Avra Portnoy, available from Amazon

Wilfrid Gordon McDonald Partridge by Mem Fox, available from Amazon

GAMES AND KITS:

Alex Toys Knot-A-Quilt Kit, available from Amazon

Apples to Apples, available from Amazon

Bridge of Self-Confidence Game for Teens, available from Selfhelpwarehouse.com

Connect Four, available from Amazon

Connie's Many Feelings, available from Amazon

Consequences, available from ChristianBook.com

Doggone Grief, available from Compassion Books

Dominoes, available from Amazon or local toy store

Glee Yahtzee, available from Amazon

I Never Forget a Face, available from Amazon

Invisible Ink Pen & UV Light, available from Amazon

Jenga, available from Amazon

Kerplunk, available from Amazon or local toy store

Lineup, available from Amazon

Marble racing game, available from Amazon or local toy store

Melissa & Doug Band in a Box, available from Amazon

On the Road to Discovery, available from ADDWarehouse.com

Sense A Bility, available from Amazon

Stare, available from Amazon

The Faces Game from Buffalo Faces, available from Amazon

The Game of Life, available from Amazon

The Game of Scattergories, available from Amazon

The Good Mourning Game, available from Creativetherapystore. com (only need coping skills cards)

The Nurturing Game, available from Selfhelpwarehouse.com

The Self Esteem Game, available from Selfhelpwarehouse.com

The Ungame, available from Amazon

Wood Senet game, available from Amazon

Zobmondo!! Would You Rather..?, available from Amazon

WEBSITES:

www.donnayoung.org/homeschooling/games/game-boards.htm, game board templates

http://esdeer.com/elephant, "Elephant in the Room" poem

http://spoonful.com/crafts/butterfly-sun-catcher, directions for making butterfly sun catcher

www.Alleghenycounty.us, Explore Your Emotions coloring book

www.Authorsden.com, "Priorities" poem

www.Centerforloss.com/downloads, downloadable activity pages for this book

www.Childhoodinterventions.blogspot.com, coping skills flashcards

www.Coloring-book.info, printable coloring book pages

www.Firstpalette.com, flower templates

www.Franklincovey.com/msb/inspired/wall, Personal mission statement examples www.friendsjournal.org/2007057, "On Listening" poem

www.Hubbardscupboard.org, Feelings Bingo

www.Kidsbutterfly.org, information on butterflies

www.Poeticexpressions.co.uk, "Remember Me" poem

www.Speechtherapygames.com, Feelings Bingo

www.squidoo.com/board-game-templates, game board templates

OTHER:

Apple

Ball, squishy/soft

Beads, several colors

Bows

Brushes for watercolors

Butcher paper

Buttons, small

Cardboard

Cardboard boxes, small, white

Cards, greeting, birthday, etc.

CD player

CDs, blank

Clay (brown, green, gray, and other colors)

Clay, hard-drying

Clothespins

Colored pencils

Construction paper, 12" x 18", colored

Construction paper, 9" x 12", colored

Cookie cutter, heart-shaped

Cotton balls, 3 sizes

Craft sticks

Crayons

Dice

DVD player

Elastic string

Fabric paint

Feathers

Felt, black

Fishing line

Floral foam

Flowerpots, small

Foam board, 8.5" x 11", black

Foam board, 8.5" x 11", white

Folding table

Framed picture

Frames, 8.5" x 11", white

Game pieces (from any game, Monopoly, Sorry, Game of Life, etc.)

Gems, plastic

Gift bags

Gift boxes

Glass mosaic tiles

Glue, hot

Glue, tacky

Glue, white

Googly eyes

Highlighters

Hole punch

Index cards, five colors

iPod speakers

Laptop computer

Linguine

Loaf of bread

Magazines

Magnetic poetry words

Magnetic wire

Markers

Marshmallows

Metallic markers

Mirror

Needle and thread

Newspaper

Pads of paper, small

Paint

Paper bags, lunch size

Paperclips

Paper plates

Paper, 8.5" x 11"

Paper, 8.5" x 11", heavy, white

Paper, large sheets

Pencils

Pens

Permanent markers

Photo covers

Ping-Pong balls

Pipe cleaners

Placemats, white

Plastic cups, clear

Play-Doh

Playing cards

Pompoms, 3 sizes

Ribbons

Rocks

Sand

Scissors

Scrapbook papers

Sculpey III Polymer Clay

Silk flowers

Socks, colored and thick

Spaghetti

Starburst candies

Stickers

Straws, non-bendable

String

Tape

Tarp

Tea lights, battery operated

Tissue paper

Toothpicks

Tootsie Pop suckers

Tupperware

Watercolors

Wire hangers

Yarn

About the Author

With thanks and help from her mother, Patricia Morrissey knew she was blessed with a calling to companion others. From age 12 through college, Pat volunteered her time at schools, children's centers, and food programs for the homeless. This commitment and training helped her to solidify her future path.

"Our deepest calling is to grow into our own authentic self-hood, whether or not it conforms to some image of who we ought to be. As we do so, we will not only find the joy that every human being seeks—we will also find our path of authentic service in the world."

PARKER J. PALMER

"Be patient toward all that is unsolved in your heart and try to love the questions themselves. Do not now seek the answers, which cannot be given you because you would not be able to live them. And the point is to live everything. Live the questions."

RAINER MARIA RILKE

Pat's main passion is helping children. Her passion for lifelong learning includes her sociology undergraduate degree, master of science degree in curriculum and instruction, and her numerous educational and counseling courses. Her thirst for knowledge and wisdom will always continue.

Pat's professional career spans more than 41 years. She was an elementary and middle school teacher, curriculum leader, and instructor of graduate classes at Cardinal Stritch, University of Wisconsin-Milwaukee, and Carroll Universities. Pat also facilitated grief support groups and was the grief support and school coordinator for Milwaukee and Waukesha counties at MargaretAnn's Place in Milwaukee.

Currently, Pat is the executive director of her own grief center, Mourning Cloak (www.mourningcloak.org). Mourning Cloak is dedicated to companioning grieving children, teens, young adults, and adults. Pat is also the current co-chair of the Southeast Wisconsin Grief Network (www.sewgn.weebly.com).

Growing up in Michigan, Pat was extremely close to her family. Her immediate family included her mother, Helen, her father, Bill, a sister, Mimi, and brother, Bill. She was also fortunate to be able to spend wonderful times with her grandparents, Papa and Grandma

Morrissey, and her grandmother, Nanie. Many of her most precious memories come from her times spent at Lake Michigan with her family and friends. Pat is very proud of her Irish heritage.

Pat is married to Tom Tews and is thrilled to be living in Port Washington, Wisconsin, one block away from Lake Michigan. She has two children, Mike and Joy. She also has two grandchildren, Emily (11) and Ashley (9). Her two cats, Jerome and Cashew, keep her warm and cozy.

Companioning the Grieving Child: A Soulful Guide for Caregivers

Renowned author and educator Dr. Alan Wolfelt redefines the role of the grief counselor in this guide for caregivers to grieving children. Providing a viable alternative to the limitations of the medical establishment's model for companioning the bereaved, Dr. Wolfelt encourages counselors and other caregivers to aspire to a more compassionate philosophy in which the child is the expert of his or her grief—not the counselor or caregiver. The approach outlined in the book argues against treating grief as an illness to be diagnosed and treated but rather for acknowledging it as an experience that forever changes a child's worldview. By promoting careful listening and observation, this guide shows caregivers, family members, teachers, and others how to support grieving children and help them grow into healthy adults.

ISBN 978-1-61722-158-3
160 pages · hardcover · $29.95

ALL DR. WOLFELT'S PUBLICATIONS CAN BE ORDERED BY MAIL FROM:

Companion
PRESS

Companion Press
3735 Broken Bow Road
Fort Collins, CO 80526
(970) 226-6050
www.centerforloss.com

A Child's View of Grief

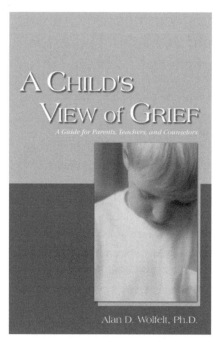

In this informative, easy-to-read booklet, Dr. Wolfelt explains how children and adolescents grieve after someone loved dies and offers helping guidelines for caregiving adults. An excellent, concise resource for parents of grieving kids.

ISBN 978-1-879651-43-2
45 pages · softcover · $6.95

ALL DR. WOLFELT'S PUBLICATIONS CAN BE ORDERED BY MAIL FROM:

Companion Press
3735 Broken Bow Road
Fort Collins, CO 80526
(970) 226-6050
www.centerforloss.com

Healing Your Grieving Heart for Kids
100 Practical Ideas

Healing Your Grieving Heart for Kids is for young and middle readers (6-12 year-olds) grieving the death of someone loved. The text is simple and straightforward, teaching children about grief and affirming that their thoughts and feelings are not only normal but necessary. Page after page of age-appropriate activities and gentle, healing guidance.

ISBN 978-1-879651-27-2
128 pages · softcover · $11.95

Healing Your Grieving Heart for Teens
100 Practical Ideas

In this compassionate book for grieving teenagers, Dr. Wolfelt speaks honestly and straightforwardly to teens, affirming their thoughts and feelings and giving them dozens of teen-friendly ideas for understanding and coping with their grief. The book also acknowledges teenagers' natural tendencies to spurn adult help while encouraging them to express their grief. Unlike longer, more text-dense books on grief, the one-idea-per-page format is inviting and readable for this age group.

ISBN 978-1-879651-23-4
128 pages · softcover · $11.95

ALL DR. WOLFELT'S PUBLICATIONS CAN BE ORDERED BY MAIL FROM:

Companion
PRESS

Companion Press
3735 Broken Bow Road
Fort Collins, CO 80526
(970) 226-6050
www.centerforloss.com

The Healing Your Grieving Heart Journal for Teens

With a Foreword by Brian Griese

Teenagers often don't want to talk to adults—or even to their friends—about their struggles. But given the opportunity, many will choose the more private option of writing. Many grieving teens find that journaling helps them sort through their confusing thoughts and feelings.

Yet few journals created just for teens exist and even fewer address the unique needs of the grieving teen. In the Introduction, this unique journal—written by Dr. Wolfelt and his then 14-year-old daughter, Megan—affirms the grieving teen's thoughts and feelings and offers gentle, healing guidance. The six central needs of mourning are explained, as are common grief responses. Throughout, the authors provide simple, open-ended questions for the grieving teen to explore, such as:

• What do you miss most about the person who died?

• Write down one special memory.

• Which feelings have been the most difficult for you since the death? Why?

• Is there something you wish you had said to the person who died but never did?

• Describe the personality of the person who died.

Designed just for grieving teens as a companion to Dr. Wolfelt's bestselling *Healing Your Grieving Heart for Teens: 100 Practical Ideas*, this journal will be a comforting, affirming, and healing presence for teens in the weeks, months, and years after the death of someone loved.

ISBN 978-1-879651-33-3 · 128 pages · softcover · $11.95

ALL DR. WOLFELT'S PUBLICATIONS CAN BE ORDERED BY MAIL FROM:

Companion Press
3735 Broken Bow Road
Fort Collins, CO 80526
(970) 226-6050
www.centerforloss.com

Educational Seminars

Come join us in Colorado for a 4-day training with Dr. Wolfelt on Helping Children and Adolescents Cope With Grief! This seminar takes a comprehensive look at a variety of subtopics related to child and adolescent mourning. Learn from one of North America's leading grief educators about:

- The major factors influencing the child's response to loss.
- Dimensions of childhood grief and helping roles.

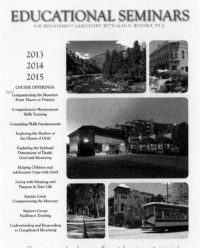

Come join us for these small-group learning experiences!

- The six central reconciliation needs of childhood mourning.
- Tools and techniques used in counseling bereaved children.
- Potential inhibitors of the child's capacity to mourn.
- Guidelines for facilitating bereaved child and adolescent support groups.
- Special considerations for the adolescent mourner.
- Identifying the "detached child."
- Referral criteria and recommended reading lists.

This course is only offered every two years starting July 2014, so be sure to register early! Call (970) 226-6050 or visit www.centerforloss.com and click on "Attend a 4-Day Training in Colorado."

Center *for* Loss
& Life Transition®

3735 Broken Bow Road
Fort Collins, CO 80526
(970) 226-6050
www.centerforloss.com